HAIGHT ASHBURY FLASHBACKS

by STEPHEN GASKIN

Ronin Publishing, Inc   Box 1035 Berkeley CA 94701

Published by
Ronin Publishing, Inc.
Post Office Box 1035
Berkeley, California 94701

Haight Ashbury Flashbacks
ISBN: 0-914171-30-5
Copyright © 1980 and 1990 by Stephen Gaskin
(originally published by The Book Publishing Company
at The Farm in Summertown, Tenneesee
in 1980 under the Title *Amazing Dope Tales*)

First Ronin printing 1990
Printed in the United States of America

Ronin Credits
Project editors: Sebastian Orfali and Beverly Potter
Typography and production: Sebastian Orfali

Book Publishing Company Credits
Paul Mandelstein, Mathew McClure, Leon Fainbuch, James Hartman,
David Long, Gregory Lowry, Jeanne Purviance, Arthur Saarinen,
Steve Solomon, Alan Bishop, Clem Fainbuch, Drury Grigsby,
Mindy McCluskey, Janet Mundo, Marcos Taquechel, Mary Wheeler,
James Egan, Nancy Holzapfel, Abert Livick, Daniel Luna,
Nancy Van Camp, Jane Ayers, Tortesa Livick, Richard Martin,
Joan McCabe, Roy Ross, Andrew Nestler, David Prentice,
John Seward, David Stitz, and Bruce Moore

Foreword to Second Edition

I saved this book for ten years to wait for the statute of limitations to run out before publication. When we at the Farm finally did publish it under the title **Amazing Dope Tales**, it landed right in the middle of the year that Jerry Falwell shut down the headshops. And it only sold about 20,000. Bookstores owners were afraid to put it on the shelves but they would buy one copy to read themselves.

As I look over these stories for this new edition, I find that they are just as fresh for me as the first time I tried to set them down. That is one of the magic things about tripping, remembering it does it to you again. When I remember the great, courageous, goodhearted trippers of Haight Street it gives me the same kind of Pity Pats of the heart that I got when that Chinese guy stepped into the street and stopped 18 tanks on their way to Tienammen Square.

I don't mind calling it **Haight Ashbury Flashbacks**, at all, because they still flash me back. In some ways they hold up better than the books that tried to be spiritual (except for **Monday Night Class**, which is history.) In my spiritual books I tried to abstract the universal and true parts of tripping for ordinary people so no one would have to think that tripping was the only way to learn.

In Flashbacks I tried to say it the way it happened. I have a couple of in-laws who both happen to be PhD microbiologists and when I gave them a copy I was trying to explain what kind of book it was and I said,

"These are a bunch of observations that were too delicate to crack out of the matrix so I had to just put them in whole."

I think it is very important for all of us who were helped so much by psychedelics to stand up for the flag and not try to pretend that we learned it all on our own with no help. In the words of an old friend, Steve Camacho,
   "When one last prayer is all I've got
   I Want to say God Bless Pot."

Stephen Gaskin
The Farm
Summertown,
Tennessee

Introduction

by Spider Robinson

"What did you do in the Sixties, Mom and Dad?"

This question is starting to be asked across the land of late. I suspect the most common response is an attempt to change the subject. We Sixties Survivors don't tend to tell our war stories much these days, and especially not to our kids.

If you can remember the Sixties," George Carlin says, "you weren't there." The joke is supposed to be that all the drugs we did back then impaired memory formation- and it must be sadly admitted that there is some truth in....in....whatever it was I just said.

But another part of our reticence is that we are made distinctly uneasy by some of our memories.

We did incredibly audacious things in those days. No, let's choose an adjective which flatters us less: we did foolhardy things in those days. We diced not only with Death, but with Madness. As we age, our memories scare us, because our children are reaching the age at which we took those risks, and we remember what we did better than we remember why we did it.

(We did it for spiritual reasons.)

(We did it because we had to.)

(We did it because it was about the only method we could find of changing our own metaprogramming that did not require a thick owner's manual and years of study and hard work- and we urgently needed to repair bad internal programming that was causing our systems to hang and our heads to crash.)

(We did it, to misquote Sir Edmund Hillary, because it wasn't there.)

But very few of us ever did anything as audacious, as potentially foolhardy, as Stephen Gaskin is doing now, in reprinting a book at this particular juncture in history.

Just a few more years, and *Haight Ashbury Flashbacks* would have moved quietly and harmlessly from the custody of archivists to that of archaeologists (and people care so little about what archaeologists know that, as I write this, a bunch of them are auctioning off Indiana Jones's bullwhip just to try and get someone to pay attention to them.). The guardians of our cultural history are just tightening down the last heavy-duty screws on the coffin lid of the Sixties, humming softly to drown out the muffled sounds from within. They've all but finished revising the dictionary so that "revolution" is something done by CD's and microwaves, "the movement" is the reason one takes Metamucil, "consciousness" is something you watch Phil Donahue to have raised, "vibes" are what Gary Burton plays, and "love" is a code word to get song lyrics about screwing past Tipper Gore. A whole generation has been raised so betrayed and bewildered it sees only the two choices of Hate All Drugs or Get Addicted to the Worst Ones, has unlearned so many lessons that polls claim a majority of us would be willing to accept random search of our homes to seek out dope traffickers; an entire cohort has reached adolescence so bland, blinkered, and boring it actually believes that to fuck, the simplest, most basic human act, is to Do a Wild Thing.

And then along comes this smiling madman Gaskin, this ex-Marine, ex-English professor, semi-retired wizard, and unregenerate holy man, this grinning shaggy spectre at the feast, this wild-eyed eye witness to unspeakable events and forgotten abominations, to tell them all about some *really* Wild Things! About days when warlocks walked the earth, and great magics were done, and forces were unleashed that changed the isostatic balance of the planetary head- why, this diehard hippie freak actually seems to glorify the use of dangerous drugs and discredited lifestyles!

This is a dangerous book, because once this little sucker slips out there into the bookstores, a few parents are going to find themselves having conversations they've long dreaded with their offspring, in which they may have to admit to their kids and thus to themselves that being a hippie was not a temporary phase they went through in college, a brief aberration in fashion trends exactly analogous to wearing Benetton shirts and Reeboks- that for a while, there, some Moms and Dads broke every rule they could find, had the audacity to scrap the moral code they were handed and build a new one from part -- that for a few weeks or months or years back in the Sixties, a number of people undertook, in heartbreaking ignorance and with splendid, pathetic courage, a great sustained earnest effort to fuse into telepathic communion, a failure so magnificent and so slapstick that we avoid thinking about it these days, because it hurts too much. And if we admit all that to our kids . . . they might just be young and stupid enough to think that the experiment could be worth repeating, just once more, with improved tools.

The source of fear is obvious. It's become a commonplace that the Eighties were a rerun of the Fifties. Apathetic students. Lousy music on the radio. Amiable nitwit nodding off in the White House while thieves loot the store. Universal belief in comforting lies. And so the obvious question is: what if the Fiftiesness of the Eighties were to trigger the Nineties into becoming another Sixties? With computers and better communications and more powerful new psychedelics.

I don't know if that will happen. I don't even know if I hope it will. This generation seems even more ignorant than my own was at the time; at least we had the habit and the love of reading, even if we did read so many silly things. Magic unleashed in ignorance is always dangerous. So many of us took advantage of all the confusion to do foolish or destructive things.

On the other hand, we did some amazingly beautiful things too. And we can't keep on the way we're going much longer. And those who don't read, won't read this book.

The number one lie about the Sixties is, Nothing Really Happened. Bullshit. A lot of things happened. You are about to read some of the more astonishing things that happened, at a time and place where truly astonishing things were commonplace, to a genuinely astonishing man.

Some younger readers may have difficulty in following

these tales at first. It's not the kind of thing that a glossary of terms in the back would help any; it's subtler than that. In a sense, to an extent, You Had To Be There. But if you find yourself thus mazed, press on; the longer you read, the more you'll find yourself understanding. To really explain physics, you have to use math; to convey what the Haight was like in the early Sixties, you have to speak Hipster. You'll pick it up.

Think of this as a collection of science fiction stories, about aliens who are like and yet interestingly unlike us, told by one of the aliens. Some of its colorful protagonists may just fit science fiction editor John W. Campbell's famous prescription for an alien: "something that thinks as well as a human . . . but not like a human."

As to the author . . . well, go to the dedication of this book, substitute "Stephen Gaskin" for "Suzuki-roshi" and "Nova Scotia" for "San Francisco" and you've pretty much got how I feel about Stephen. He was there at the start and at the very heart of the nova that was the Sixties, and somehow miraculously emerged relatively unsinged, in a stable orbit, with his honor and his good humor intact. Maybe there is some justice after all. As long as he is loose with a Macintosh and a laser printer, no bullshit anywhere on the planet is safe.

I ask any who find this book outrageous to note clearly that nowhere in it are heroin, cocaine, PCP, alcohol, crack, or their like spoken of with approval -- that these are tales not of dope that makes you stupid, but of dope that makes you think, and go beyond thinking. Note too that the dangers inherent in even those drugs are delineated here with merciless clarity. The stupidities of the time are here on display right alongside the shining insights. If the Sixties ever should return, careful study of this volume might well help prevent the repeating of some painful mistakes.

This is an oral history of one of the most incredible times in human history; read and wonder.

> *- Vancouver, B.C.*
> *June,1990*

(Spider Robinson is an award-winning science fiction writer; somehow or other Stephen Gaskin has managed to creep into at least four of his twelve books, most recently *Time Pressure*)

I didn't know Suzuki Roshi, but I was slightly acquainted with him. I sat with him once or twice, and went to hear him lecture a few more times. But I didn't have to go see him all the time, or spend a lot of time in his presence: He had his integrity whether I was there or not.

Knowing that he was there and that he had his integrity all the time made it so that I felt safe. As wild and scary and trippy as it was in San Francisco, I felt safe, because I knew there was such a thing as an honest man. I knew an honest man. I knew where an honest man lived. I knew I could go see him and talk to him if I wanted to. There was an honest man there who believed in reality. He was the strength to all of my trippings: Everything I ever did in San Francisco was strengthened from knowing that he was there, that he existed, that he was like he was.

And I find that I tend to respect him more rather than less as time goes on, as I see how long it takes to find another one like that.

Table of Contents

Introduction

 arly on, way back in my earliest trips, I felt like acid was something I understood instinctively, and was good at, and was going to continue to be good at. I always knew from the very first times I tripped that I just *dug it.* I loved it. It seemed—not exactly *easy* to do, but it seemed like the only really *natural* thing that I'd ever done in my life. It was like someone who was a good swimmer, but had lived where there was never any water, and the first time you

1

threw him in the water he could swim. I loved it, and I've loved it ever since, and I'll always love it.

It seemed like we were in a time machine where time was really accelerated. We were learning *fast*. We had to learn everything we could learn as fast as we could learn it; and nearly anything we did was cool in a sense, because it was *all learning*; whatever happened to you hardly mattered, as long as you paid attention and tried not to hurt anybody. It was all paying attention; and you couldn't build experiments fast enough to catch acid. You just had to blunder on through and take notes.

I used to read a lot—I always liked weird science fiction and strange stuff when I was a kid so I was well primed with some weird things to blow up when I tripped. By the time I was thirteen, I was sure that there was no magic, and I was chasing telepathy through Dr. Rhine, the ESP researcher, which was way back up there in the odds: an awfully slow, pedestrian way to do it, I thought. My concept of thought and telepathy was always swifter than that.

I liked Huxley. At first I read his novels: *Chrome Yellow, Point Counter Point, Eyeless in Gaza,* and all that kind of stuff. Then I heard he went mysto, and I thought he was sold out. Later on, *I* went mysto, and looked him up again. Then I read *Doors of Perception* and books like that for a year or two before I actually tripped. I was aware of acid and thinking about it, and reading good books, or what I thought were good books, coming down to it, thinking I would probably do it some day.

Huxley was interesting, but not making any sense. I can remember reading about words like *transcendence*, that were just meaningless to me at the time. And now I look back through that kind of thing, and those factors are like the weather, sort of a topological map of the existing astral plane. The question is not one of *understanding* transcendence; it's of *transcending,* it's *experiencing* transcendence.

I began to suspect that there was something more there

than met the eye. His writings in *Doors of Perception* were strange.

Then, when I got stoned and found myself giggling about philosophical concepts of reality, I understood Huxley a lot better.

We got very *sensitive* from tripping that much and working to clear our circuits that much. I could be in the living room reading a book, and feel that somebody was smooching and getting it on in the other end of the house; and I could walk to the other end of the house, and sure enough, there would be somebody smooching. I would just feel that vibe wash through me, and light up all my electricity. It would feel just like somebody getting it on, somebody smooching. It was a warm, lovely, sexy feeling, projected down a long San Francisco shotgun flat, some fifty or sixty feet.

That vibration was projected through a medium. One CB radio, a little five-watt spark in Tennessee, can so excite the medium that it can be heard in Guatemala: the electronic medium is incredibly responsive, much more responsive than the material plane solids, wood, steel, glass, wires.

Perfectly coupled nothing.

You take a little nothing over here, and you couple it to a little nothing over there.

When we were first telepathic, we were always trying to prove it. I would go to the cafeteria and sit down and just freak people out.

"Can you feel this?"

I remember I was out with this guy who used to be a teacher of mine. I was talking with him and he said,

"You know? This is kind of weird. I think I *do* feel something!" And he took off and walked away from me as fast as he could.

After some time of that sort of thing, I decided to stop seeking outside affirmation. I started having my proofs built out of circumstance rather than trying to go and zap people

3

and ask them if they felt it.

At first, it was trying to make experiments to catch acid. Then I learned that you just watch the flow; the experiments will all work themselves out before your very eyes. The only reason we even have the concept of experiments is that some people who observed for a long time and saw a lot of cause and effect happen, then, for the convenience of other people, put those into little bundles as if they had happened together, and called them experiments.

There is a certain point when you know *you're tripping all the time now.* For a long time, every time I came down, I felt like I'd sinned, or I wouldn't have come down.

And that's true. But it isn't anything to be uptight about. The miracle is that there's a trampoline at all, not that there's some of it that springs down and some of it that springs up.

The folks I mention in this book are my friends. My contemporaries, for sure, but most of them are my friends, actually. These are the folks I *tripped with.* Folks you tripped with are like the folks you went through your initiation with. Even if you fought all the way through the trip, later on, just that you were on it together is more important than whether you fought during it or not, or whether you even liked each other at the time.

Those folks were the revolution in a lot of ways, and the power that came out of their thing informed and powered a tremendous amount of the civil rights and the anti-war movements. I think these people are worthy of great respect, and should be proud of what they were, even if they later cut their hair.

There's a lot of folks very *impressed* who did not realize that there were events going down which had *impressive* qualities and *imprint* potentialities, and that you had to be watching. The reason that I have this stuff in my head is that I was really trying to pay attention. I really didn't want anybody to be putting a lot of stuff in my head that I didn't

4

notice going in, when I was that stoned, because I instinctively understood that I was just a blank tablet.

Acid was like that game where you have five minutes in the supermarket to fill your basket. It's like you have ten square feet of canvas, and x number of acid trips to fill it. You just run and paint—and at some time, you'll settle down and look at what you painted. It's like that run in the supermarket: you just grab a handful, stripe a splash of color, and haul ass.

Some of the people who could do some very fancy psychic stuff have lost faith in dope and don't trip anymore, and have forgotten stuff that has changed my mind in ways I can never forget, even though *I haven't taken any acid in ten years.* Some of the guys I did those trips with are just *gone.* They forgot and went square, a little because of money and their families; but for many of them, they messed around with the wrong kind of magic so much that they just lost their juice.

Folks used to play fierce games. They used to deal acid, while *on* acid. Big deals, gram deals, thousands of hits. They would deal while they were stoned, and have really heavy power trips about the price, while *stoned*, which is a gross misuse of the power. You can see why they lost their powers, using it like that. Lost their powers from messing around.

And there ain't many of us from that crop who still have any powers left.

5

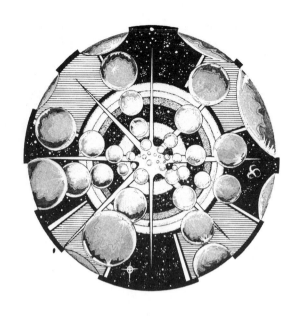

Turning On

hen I was seventeen and in the Marine Corps, I went and visited my cousin who lived in California. He had been smoking grass for a while, himself, and he wanted to turn me on. It was a good impulse, in a way, but he got a little carried away with it.

We got in the car, and went out on a lonely beach. We stood on the sidewalk by the sand, and burned this joint together.

He wanted to be sure I got high. He had me take a long,

strong toke, and then squat down and blow on my thumb. After a few of those, he had me floating and really banged. Then he took me back to the car.

As we were walking back to the car, we came to the curb. I stopped at the curb for a moment, and looked down at it.

"Look down over the edge," my cousin said. "Look at the rapids. See the white water breaking around the rocks— *waayyy* down there at the bottom of the canyon, where the rapids are."

While I was looking at that, as he was telling me to, he walked around behind me and pushed me off the curb.

I fell six inches, and landed stiff-kneed, jolting every vertebra I had from landing that way, because I was not at all ready to land in six inches.

He thought that was funny, and took me off in the car. As we drove off down the road I said,

"Take it easy, it's my dad's car."

"Hee-hee-hee," he said. "I'm going to drive fast. I'm going to drive *fast. Ah hah! You see how fast I'm driving? I'm going to drive* **real fast!** *I'm going to drive fast, and scare you!* **I'm going to drive really fast!**" And it seemed to me that we were going *very* fast.

He jacked me up and got me very nervous and weird over that we were going to go fast. But while he was doing that, he never went over about twenty-five or thirty miles an hour.

Then we stopped and parked somewhere, just to hang out and trip together for a while. He said,

"You know, I can just control you. I can make you high and I can bring you down. I can lift you up and I can bring you down."

He started telling me that, and I said,

"Aw, come on, you can't either," and things like that.

He started telling a bunch of jokes and saying funny things, and he got me stoned and giggling and high. And all

7

of a sudden he said something to me real gross and unkind. Just cut me off short and froze me up.

"See? I can bring you down. I can get you high."

While I was still sitting there trying to digest that, he got me to where I could laugh again. He got me back up. But I never trusted him again. I couldn't, after that; and I identified that with grass for a long time.

We got home—we were staying at his house. I went in, and I had the most incredible raid of the icebox that I have ever had in my entire life. I went into that icebox and had a chicken leg in one hand, and was schlumping up cold mashed potatoes. I was eating peas that were stuck together with glops of frozen margarine. I ate a long time; just indiscriminately eating everything on two shelves of that refrigerator, before I slowed down enough. I thought, *That was really fun.* That was the first feed I'd ever been on—my first *feast.* The first time I ever enjoyed eating to that extent. It was just delightful. It was a real help to me, because I was a skinny non-eater.

But I was afraid, because of what he had done to me. He had violated the Guide position.

I didn't understand that at the time. All I knew was that something wrong had been done to me, and that I was not going to do grass again.

Grass Again

en years later I really turned on. It was with a good dude who was one of my real early teachers. George was an artist and art history student. Not in college, necessarily, although he took some college courses. But he was an artist already, as well as a student of art. He had some *beautiful* old art books, and he showed me ancient art with folks with mushrooms floating over their heads. He showed me that in many cases, the auras of saints were designed to look like a mushroom, or to imply that the mushroom had something to do with that. He showed me all these ancient paintings of an obviously psychedelic religious feeling. He was really a student of religion, too. He looked French, had *long* hair, before most folks did.

He turned me on to my first successful grass. It was my birthday, and a bunch of my friends were giving me a party. It was real nice and friendly, and George came and brought a little carved German pipe, with some kind of little face on it, and a little top. He loaded me up on Acapulco Gold, and said,

"Just take a good hit of this."

"I ain't really done any of this," I said.

"You do this," he said.

He was such a nice guy, and I liked him so much, that I just did it, although I had been *fried* ten years ago when I had last tried it.

We got all *stoned*, and I knew he was too, and every time I'd look into his eye, I'd see it looking back out at me, and it would make us both laugh. I was very telepathic with him, just right there together. At some point I got so telepathic that I said,

"Man! I feel so *telepathic* with you! Do you feel like that?"

"Yes! Yes! It's where it's at, man! Ain't it neat?"

There is a kind of tequila called *tequila almendrada* that's yellow and golden colored. It felt like I had a *tequila almendrada* yellow filter on—yellow and goldy everything.

I just *cruised* through that night. And in the morning, I felt *good*; there was no hangover, like I usually had from boozing, because I hadn't boozed. I'd forgotten to drink because I was so delighted to be stoned. I thought,

I'm probably not going to drink very much any more.

And I'm probably going to do this a lot.

One Toke Poke

ne time I was over at George's house. There were a few people there, smoking a little dope. He came over to me and said,

"This is good hash. You can get off on this hash." He filled me up a pipeful of it, and said,

"Here's what you do. Squat down on the floor and stick the pipe in your mouth, and stand up as you suck."

I lit up, expanded my chest, stood up straight and sucked

in as hard as I could on that pipe full of hash. I sucked in all I could stand—I had over seven liters lung capacity when I was measured in college, and I totally loaded it up with hash on that toke.

He took the pipe out of my hand, and I fell back into this chair.

The last thing I remember seeing in this world was when I looked over and there was a bowl from Mexico, the kind with scratchings and scorings in the bottom to grind up your garlic on. These scratches and scorings were worn smooth and thin until the pattern was clear gone in the bottom.

As I looked into the bowl, and followed the pattern around, I fell through the bottom of the bowl, where the pattern wasn't complete. It was like a hole in the bottom of a basket, and I just fell on out.

I fell out into nowhere, and nothing, for a while.

No sound. No memory. No thought.

Then I began to hear sounds around me, but I couldn't recognize them.

I began to feel sensations with my body.

Then I realized that the sounds were voices, but I didn't know what they were saying.

Then the voices became clearer, and began to make sense, and I began to realize that these were people I knew, and that I was here, at this party, and that I had taken this hit on this hash, and...

Then, when I realized that, I slid back into myself like sliding down a slide—*sssshunck!* Right up into myself in one chunk when I got that close. But I managed to sneak up to it real close before the gravitational field got me and sucked me into the gravity well, into myself.

I was gassed on the fine realization I'd had coming back in. I didn't know what to call it at the time, but it cleaned me like a bath in my mind. I felt clean and good.

Then later on, down the line, I learned to call that an

ego death. And I realized that I'd had an ego death and rebirth on one toke of hash.

Dynamite Reefer

I remember the first time I saw a hallucination, the first time I ever understood what a hallucination *was*. I realized that a hallucination didn't have to be anything radically different from what was there, to be a hallucination. It only has to be *very subtly* different.

I was sitting out in a little grape arbor in a swing, carving a bowl for a pipe out of a piece of bamboo, for a water pipe. Just as I got the bowl carved and stuck into the top of the pipe, this guy arrives with a bunch of Acapulco Gold.

My old lady at that time was attempting to make fudge in the kitchen. She came outside to hang out and smoke dope while the fudge was cooking. We fired up a pipeful of all this Acapulco Gold.

Suddenly, everything broke loose. The whole picture broke loose and got malleable, and started floating. I started seeing that some people looked a little *funny*. I could see the subconscious on people.

My vision got so good that it caused everybody to just sort of *scatter* all of a sudden. It just broke up the scene. The fudge turned out to be chocolate soup, and by that time we were so stoned and decadent that we ate it in bowls with spoons. It was grand. *Good* grass.

That's what got me my first hallucination, was Acapulco Gold. It's like the Rastafarians say, you really don't need acid, because *dynamite reefer make you trip*. That's what this one dude in dredlocks told me.

Pop Culture

hen I was in college, I hardly read anyone who was alive—that's what you do in college, because everyone in the English Department is so competitive that none of them can agree on anyone who is alive, because they think they're better than all the living ones.

I started tripping with Charlie and Linda and Paul and John and Bob and Kemo and them guys. We went over to this house, and it was far out. Charlie and Linda lived there together, just lived together. It blew my mind. They were one of the first young couples I'd met who just lived together. I was from square country.

They had lots of rock 'n' roll records, and they had lots of comic books. They had Doc Strange, a whole box, all in order. And they had a whole box of Fantastic Four, all in order. And they had a whole box of Thor, all in order. They had a *lot* of comic books.

There was a lot of pop philosophy coming out in the comic books at that time. They pointed out to me that comic books had changed: it used to be that they were very stick-figured like Superman and Lois Lane; but in the Fantastic Four, the characters had *personalities*, and *interacted*. They hassled with each other, and had problems and phobias and stuff; they had to conquer themselves to do things. Doc Strange had to do a lot of self-conquering. The battles he fought were not always something outside that could be done with a *savate* kick: he had to come in and get to himself inside. It was said that some of that continuity was being written by acid-takers. I don't know if that was true, but that's what was being said. And we believed it, because it looked like it.

So they were running all this pop culture, and they would use metaphors from comic books in their trips. On acid trips, they'd talk about how *this was just like when Thor happened across the bridge in Valhalla when Loki and Thor were having it out.*

I hung out and got stoned with these kids, and listened to the Who play *Boris the Spider*, and had it about scare me up my tree. *Boris the Spider* was *scary*, I realized. And the Who was even scary, some.

They taught me the Tolkien trilogy. They told me about Gandalf the Grey.

These were people who were students where I was teaching. We talked about magic and telepathy of every form. We went through and combed all of our experiences, and talked about it together. They were my first tripping partners, and some of my first teachers.

17

Number Six: Blue Sandoz

here was a dealer friend of mine, who had two handles: Ulysses S. Grant and Vulcan. He used to cruise Haight Street in an army coat with epaulets in his Ulysses S. Grant incarnation. He also carried a four-point in political science and sociology at San Francisco State, and looked like William Bendix, who played the *Life of Reilly.* He was a bigger, older, slightly balding, thick, heavy-duty guy, to be around all those young guys in the college like that.

I wanted some acid, and I knew he had some, so I went over to his place to get some from him. This was back in the early days, and there weren't any dealers around, so you got it through friends. What he had was a little blue cap, a very small blue cap, and he said,

"This is Sandoz."

He said it really respectfully.

I went home with that little blue cap, and I dropped it. I was with two friends of mine, David Smith, a poet, and Paul H. I don't know where they were at, because I just laid back and relaxed. I heard them talking kind of over in the corner of my mind, when I started slipping into myself, into my own thing.

Then I was looking from over a view of a little creek that was very bright yellow, running down over the rocks. I looked at it, and there were bubbles on it. And suddenly I was one of the bubbles on the creek, running down this little golden river.

I bounced around a few times, and then I popped.

My bubble popped, and then I was indistinguishably part of the river.

And I don't know anything for hours, except for vague memories of feeling good and bright lights. For hours.

When I came drifting back in from that, David and Paul were still there and still talking, and it was like I had been on subjective time for years and years. I came back into their conversation.

That was one of the only times I ever went somewhere else than the people I was with, and didn't relate with them.

There was no verbal content, no semantic content. That was sort of like a benchmark for me for acid's ego death.

There was no messing around, being-dragged-kicking-and-screaming or any of that.

It's hard on you to get about halfway there, and have your ego kicking and screaming and raising hell, and try to get over it, and not have enough juice to get over it, and not have enough power under your belt to give you any faith.

If you have enough on, even if your ego's acting up, you can get lost enough in the magic and the beauty of it that you can't think about yourself anyway. It'll just push you right over.

I don't mind chipping when I know I'm chipping—that was what we called just biting off a corner of a tab just for the buzz; but I don't like to chip when I think I'm tripping. When I want to trip, I want to *trip*.

San Francisco State: Early Trips

 here was a dude who ran the classic acid/speed power trip at San Francisco State College. He was a teacher named Mac-something. When he started tripping, he thought,

Why not have a revolution of the mind, and change the world?

And he got very serious, and kind of uptight about it. I think the reason he began to get weird was that he was keeping his juice up with Dexedrine while taking lots of acid and not eating very much, getting skinny and emaciated and wild and weird looking—as somebody is who is taking a bunch of acid and speed all the time.

He ran one of the classic games. These are like the classic openings in chess—like Piano or something. He up and produced some grass in class, and turned on the class one day.

He turned them on, and the word got out to the Administration. The Administration crapped. They started coming on to him. And instead of backing it down, he stuck to it, and turned them on again. He began to bet that *this was going to be the beginning of the revolution*—that he was going to confront the college head-on and the ante would be up enough and the people would back him because he was bucking the system. Classic power trip.

He got into that, and was getting weirder and talking weirder. When you would talk with him, he would give you the classic kind of speech which people like that have. They are always talking to themselves in their mind, proving their point as if arguing with somebody, rehearsing lines they are going to use when they find somebody to use them on. So they're going along kind of blustering along, arguing their point in their mind all the time. It makes them have serious, knit-browed expressions, and look all *consternated*, as Margaret says.

They also present their case in an airtight, Aristotelian logical sequence, where they say,

"If I do this, then they'll do that; then if I do this, they'll do that; and if I do *this*, they're going to do *that*."

It follows a very linear sequence about what has to happen and what's going to happen, and how he's going to stand them all off. And the Administration's saying,

"Back it down! Why should we have a big stink at San Francisco State College?"

And he's saying,

"If you push me, I'm going to tell the reporters. I'll tell the reporters that I'm turning them on in the classroom, and that you're not saying anything about it because you're afraid it will get out."

Classic power trip.

And the administration is getting hot, and there are several ultimatums presented and not met, and it is getting hotter and hotter. He is getting skinnier and skinnier, and talking more and more funny, and not eating much, and taking a lot of Dexedrine. And it comes up to where he is going to cop or they aren't going to goof around. They are just going to call the heat and have him arrested. It comes up to that meeting, and he has this speech in his mind to tell them guys, man. And he's going to go in there and tell them...and he don't show up. Nobody hears from him for quite a while, until somebody hears that he's bagged the whole thing, gone back to college in a different school, is toeing the line, has short hair, is not goofing around, is attempting to get a teaching job: at the very moment of truth, he looked and he saw the abyss yawning below him. He backed it right down and backed up and went and did another thing. He was turned around by acid. Acid didn't let him do it. But it led him right up to the edge.

There were always these people going around on these power trips. I didn't used to pay my parking tickets, because I figured the government would fall before it went to warrant. It was imminent, man.

And everybody really thought they were going to do that, start a revolution right there from that point. Kesey was going to do that. Grogan was going to do that. Leary was going to do that. Everybody was going to do that. That was the thing everybody thought you could do, that there would be a quick reversal turnaround of the whole thing.

And the funny thing is, there was.

Attorney General Mitchell stood up there and watched them herd anti-war demonstrators into the football field without warrants or formal charges, and said,

"This country's going to go so right-wing you wouldn't recognize it."

And it didn't.

The school board of the City of Nashville is voluntarily figuring out an integration plan. They hate it. They are having a hard time doing it. But they are doing it. Doing it, in neckties, and civilly. Nixon didn't get to finish his term, and we got out of Viet Nam.

There *was* a big turnaround. Viet Nam was so wrong that it kept this country having a conscience for several years. Up until recently.

So many people turned around that it threw out a vibe through the whole country. There were many people who were willing to go to some lengths to make themselves heard. There were many people who were devoutly into the juice. That was the real religion of the country for a while, *into the juice.* High church, low church.

I was pretty neurotic. There were several pretty neurotic guys there, who were all making good grades. They gave good grades and a masters' degree to a guy who, when he got his first phone call from a job interview at Berkeley, the college said,

"Well, actually this guy is crazy, and it would be better if you didn't have him. He actually needs psychiatric help."

They never said anything to him, all the way through graduate school. Nobody ever said anything to him about it. They gave him a Master's degree and sent him out, and the *first time* anybody asks for a reference, that's what they got.

I tripped with that guy. His name was O. He was tall and skinny, and he wore a black suit, all the time, the same one, and a green tie, and kind of a yellowed shirt, pretty much the same one all the time. He wore it the same way people wear jeans: he slept in it, he drank in it, he fought and barfed in it, he took acid in it—it was his clothes. It was his black suit. He had serious acne.

I did not understand the permutations of the agony of the ego. I just thought he was weird. But he was *smart*. He was really smart, and he was telepathic with me in a lot of ways. But really not at all in other ways.

He went to graduate school, and was a teaching assistant in people's courses, and taught classes, for which you would think a high level of integration is required. I tell you that this crazy guy did it, and nobody said anything.

I was crazy, too, but not quite as crazy as him. He and I and S. all began into dope together. And he and S. got weird together. And I knew it. And O. knew I knew it. And he was always after my head. He was so crazy all the time, that he understood the acid ground rules instinctively. When I would be a couple of hours into some good acid, with a few friends, quietly playing games like turning up the colors for each other, this cat would knock on the door—and just like some people know the exact thing to say to get into a mental institution, this cat knew exactly what clauses of the Universal Code to invoke so that I could not cast him, a fellow soul, out onto the street, and I would have to take him in. He really knew how to do that. I would say, from sailing along an hour and a half into some good acid,

"Come in, O." Knowing that he was implacably into the juice, on a Gothic pride trip, seriously unlaid, possibly terminally unlaid.

I realized he was doing the same thing to S. He turned S. down on me. S. still writes me crazy mail. "You said you were a writer, and you sold out." "Don't think I don't know some people are following me." "Boy, you better not come around me and follow me, or I might blow you away." Real, seriously paranoid. Planted by O. But S. was my good friend and I loved him, and I felt really bad when he went sour on me and I couldn't get it on with him any more.

S. was a funny kind of obsessive personality anyway. He

wrote good stories, but he'd take off on a novel or a story and get one vignette in it, and then he would just expand that into a whole new thing and forget his novel. Which I guess is all right, you follow where your pen leads; it's the only way to write, if you're going to be a writer, I suppose. But he never finished anything. He just did that and did that and did that. And the one he was on was always a gasser, and the last one he didn't put any value into anyway.

He married a nice girl. I said something about,

"You guys ought to be hippies."

She said, "Aw, we're real hippies, Stephen. We've been on welfare for *months*."

O. would always come over and ask me,

"How do you do your stuff? Where do you get your juice?"

I'd tell him a lot of different stuff, because he came over a lot of times. Sometimes I would show him how the book I was reading right now had some of that in it—if I was studying the Tarot, I'd say "This is how the Tarot talks about it," and explain it that way.

And every time, somewhere in there I would get around to the idea of being responsible for the creation of your own character. Just as a notion. And every time I would come to that place, he would say,

"Don't hand me all that old bullshit. How come you always give me all that old bullshit when I ask you where you get your stuff?" He would always come on cynical. And I would say,

"No, man, I ain't putting you on. I ain't doing weird rites in the night and not telling you."

O. was an intimidator. He's one of the guys from whom I learned that a black magician has his toolkit, too: for every thing a white magician has, a black magician has something in his kit that serves that same purpose for him. Whether or not it is decent or lawful to use it, it is something that serves that purpose. Where a very high swami or yogi might be

26

said to be above desire or unattached about how things come out—affectionately detached—somebody like O. just *didn't give a shit*. And that covered the same ground for him. And where somebody might have to really study Zen or Raja yoga and have great insights to understand the secret of space and time, somebody might just *not keep track*.

He was the kind of guy who knew how to throw out one of those numbers like,

Well, you ain't so cool, yourself.

That's a really cheap and easy way to put the screws to somebody. It's one of the pieces of a black magician's toolkit, because it's specific. It works best on people who care. If you don't care, it can't do anything to you. But if you care, and are like most human beings in that you wouldn't be able to snap to and say exactly where you were at at any instant, being a grownup and for the sake of argument, you'd have to admit that maybe you ain't too cool right now. But once O. would drop it on you that you weren't too cool, there was nothing else you could say.

He'd start these philosophical arguments which would lead out into nowhere, and quit, because they were actually specious. He'd put you on, on purpose, and rip you off; and when you'd decide that you'd about had it with him, and were about to boot him, he'd say,

"Got to split, man."

He'd come around and act like he was crazy and in need of help. And when you would offer him help, he would suck you in and suck you in until he got you out of shape. And then he would pop it on you again, that he was putting you on some more.

The last time I saw O. was when we were coming down Haight Street in our schoolbus. I saw him at a bus stop about a block down the road, in his first costume change. He had gone to a black leotard-y thing and a dirty looking mustard ochre colored cloak. He looked back up and saw my bus and recognized me, and turned his head away from me, and

27

continued to rotate and keep his back to me as we came by. He didn't look so I could see his face. I never saw him again. It was like he came out for a curtain call in his black costume and ochre coat. Kind of like the green necktie color, almost. Scabrous old costume again, too. Raunchy and dirty looking.

Patrick G. was one of us tortured teachers at the time. The way he got free was that he also gave up teaching. He became a musician and followed synthesizers and recording as a discipline. I have seen a recent picture of him, and his face looks at peace. He does not look like the driven, Saint John the Baptist, head on a platter, dude that he used to be.

He was just starting with the Moog when I knew him. He said teaching and writing was not doing it for him, and went off in this other direction. And it seems to have been a good one for him.

He was an enormously smart and talented cat. He was the guy who, when he was hired at San Francisco State College, the English Department said,

"Lookie here. We know he's a Ph.D., but he's got long hair. If we're going to hire hair, don't you think we ought to have at least a published novel?"

That was said. I wasn't there when it went down; but that's what was said.

Anyway, he was a hotshot. He wrote his doctorate in thirty days.

I shared an office with him. He told me one time,

"I intend to show myself a good time over the next several months, and I might invite you along for the companionship of it."

I said, "Sure. Let's roll."

So we did stuff like rent a houseboat in the Sacramento River Delta and go mess around for the weekend.

I would go over to his house and see him sometimes, and he would always surprise me, because he was such a far out dude.

I had come through Death Valley once. I said,

"Man, it was *hot* in Death Valley."

He said, "It's not that bad in Death Valley."

"Patrick, have you ever *been* to Death Valley?"

"Why, yes. I spent thirty days in a loincloth in Death Valley as an Air Force survival instructor."

We used to argue about dope. He'd tell me he preferred DMT, and I'd tell him that I preferred acid. I thought you were responsible for more, longer on acid; you could get into quite a bit of trouble on DMT, but you'd come down so quick that you wouldn't have any thing really *committing* happen to you, when you were only up such a short time. I thought that being up for six or eight hours put you into a higher level of commitment about things.

So he was a tripper, too. It wasn't that he wasn't a magician. I don't see how somebody can be an English major and a pretty talented sketch artist...

There was this girl whom he and I both loved, who actually never tumbled for either of us. She was the girl who moved in upstairs from me on Mission Street. She was a nice, hippie lady. I was still teaching at college—I was under no pretensions, even, of hipness. I didn't understand what it was.

She had a graceful hippy way. To me she was the epitome of the hippy woman culture of the sixties. She had this pad on top of the roof with windows all around it with sunlight coming in; a few crystals hanging in the windows, and a few plants growing in the windows, and everything bright and sunny, with bright and sunny colors. She wore Gibson-girl old-fashioned hairdo's, and wore old-fashiony kind of clothes sometimes; but it was not the shopping bag lady look; it was more a neo-Victorian that was very neo. It was very hip. She was really a nice lady, and he drew a sketch of her once. He did her bellbottoms in one line, and he had the shape of her motion so cold in that line that it was plain that he was a good artist, and it was plain that he had excellent eye/hand coordination, and it was plain that he loved her. Just in the line that was the outside of the shape of her bellbottoms.

But he didn't last. He fell out of wanting to do it with the English Department, and he fell out of wanting to do it with academic things whatsoever. He designed furniture for a while. He designed a couch for which the end pieces were inch-and-a-half-thick Plexiglas, about four foot squares standing on edge at each end of the couch; and everything in between that was crushed brown velvet. And he used to tell me he loved plastic when I was down on plastic.

"Plastic beats critters," he said.

I dig what he meant, too.

I learned about social class for the first time in my life through taking acid while I was still teaching in the English Department of San Francisco State College. Nothing had ever really happened to me before that had brought home what social class was, before then. I had gone to any level of anything I had ever wanted to; I had never identified with any of it, and nothing had ever harmed me. I had not been soiled or dirtied by anything I had ever touched. I was quite naive.

I came to realize that the faculty was like a club. If you weren't going to get in the club, you weren't going to get in the club. And it didn't matter—anything didn't matter. If you weren't going to get in the club, you weren't going to get in the club. It took me a while to understand that. And as I took more dope, I began to understand.

Even though I was teaching five classes at San Francisco State College, I was not a member of the faculty. I was just not a member of it.

I was teaching general semantics and creative writing, as well as a bunch of Freshman English, which was what everybody started on. I was very lucky to have creative writing and general semantics courses, and not just all bonehead English.

I never understood before, and then I understood that there is such a thing as a certain level of social class, and that if you didn't hit it just right, it wasn't going to do it. I was like a monkey walking into the monolith from *2001* in the woods: *What is this object?* I smelled it and bit it on the sides a little, to see what it was. And I realized for the first time that my family was not what you would call a middle class family by American standards of middle class.

I had never considered that. We owned our own home wherever we went; my father did lots of interesting stuff, like be a commercial fisherman in California for a while, and own a house trailer business for a while in Denver, and have a chicken-ranch business for a while in Santa Fe.

My father had what passed for an executive job during World War II. He had four secretaries, and made $3600 a year. They said,

"Okay, we have a bigger base with a larger job down in Tucson, Arizona, for you to go to. Go on down, and you can take over as General Housing Manager for that base."

We took off down there, and got there in the middle of the night. We went to several motels, and none of them were open. My father said,

"You know, it don't look like Tucson wants us. And if Tucson don't want us, I don't think we want Tucson."

We just filled up and drove on out to California, and chucked the whole government job trip, the entire thing. Just didn't report to work at that place, and went to be a commercial fisherman in California.

He found a man who was leaving California because he was afraid the Japanese were going to invade. I met several people out there who were serious about that question. This cat sold us a beautiful house on Balboa peninsula and a forty-foot teak and mahogany twin-Chrysler marine engine cabin cruiser, very cheap.

My father was a good carpenter, and he took the back two cabins off the cabin cruiser and put in a weather deck with scuppers, and we went mackerel fishing. We had one of the fastest boats in the mackerel fishing fleet. He was independent as could be. I'd watch him fold up a whole business, owning property, everything, just fold it all up, put it in a money belt, and drive to another place and start over. I didn't understand social class.

S. and O. and I all shared the same writing instructors. S. got into the old men reminiscing story. We used to sit and talk about short stories and things like that. Me and S. and O. and Mike and Tim and Fred were all in competition for the available teacher assistant jobs when we were all going to graduate school together. Fred's the one who said, "Where there's dope, there's hope."

S. was a small dude. We always referred to him as Pogo with the soft brown eyes. He was a Jewish cat from the South, and had a particular kind of sense of humor that a Jewish cat from the South can develop, which is kind of sweet, and I really enjoyed him that way. He also had roots back to the Bronx and back to Miami. He was from folks who had gone from the Bronx to Miami. That's why he had a good feeling for the old men playing baseball. That was the story that he kept following out more and more, what they said to one another, and the Proustian evocations of the old people's life that came out through the badmouth and holler of the old men's softball game. He was a very soulful dude, the kind of stuff he was interested in that he tried to write.

There were a couple of guys the same time I was teaching at San Francisco State who all seemed to be in on the same sweepstakes. It was as if we were all going to...it was like the place of *Let the games begin*, as the billboard in San Francisco said. We all knew it was a volatile medium and something was happening; but the thing is, a lot of people had preconceived ideas of what was going to happen. One was a faculty cat who was kind of hip, kind of smart and fun to be around. He'd smoke a little dope with me, maybe drink a little beer and go out and stop in a bar and shoot the breeze about something philosophical once in a while, and then I began to be a hippy and began to get serious and stoned and a little weird.

I invited him to go do this number with me one time, and he said,

"You don't understand, man. I'm going to be around here. There's grocery stores up in North Beach with my name on the front of them. I *live* here in San Francisco. I just can't go off on this trip with you. Sorry, but that's the way it goes."

He just cut me loose, and let me go. Because he was permanent staff in San Francisco. He was not one of the hippies who was just passing through.

So that was how some people were about weird and messy dropouts.

I started going out with Margaret and started wearing a long fringe coat, and long hair and boots. I went over to see my old English teacher who had been my creative writing instructor. His wife was there, a Jewish lady who had survived Hitler's concentration camps, and when she saw how I was dressed, she took one look and said,

"You haff gone too far."

They couldn't hack me no more. I had gone too far.

33

John Scorn of Scorn's Bay

argaret and I had bought an old '53 Volkswagen bus that had been sold by the United Parcel Service for being used up. I took the top off of it and built it into a stand-up camper and we were going to go to Europe. We left San Francisco and took off to Europe, by way of Mexico and British Honduras. We thought we could take a trip down through there and then ship out from a southern port. So we got all the way down through Mexico.

It was a beautiful trip in the bus—although the crossing of Yucatan peninsula was awesome: a journey of 200 miles of low-gear on not-even-bulldozed road, but just macheted natural jungle floor. Hurricanes were whipping across the black swamps. There was another hurricane down into British Honduras, after we'd made it across onto an asphalt road eight feet wide with four inch bumps through a swamp.

By the time we got to Belize, we were totally exhausted. We had no money. We began to sell the bus equipment for a few dollars at a time. We made a serious mistake when we sold our mattress; we thought we would be shipping out in a short time on a boat.

British Honduras had about a hundred thousand people. Almost fifty thousand of them were blacks brought from Africa to work the cane fields; another fifty thousand of them were Mayan Indians, the original inhabitants; and the remaining five thousand or so were Englishmen. Indians from India were also brought into the labor force.

It was obvious that the people smoked a lot of grass in British Honduras. We quickly drifted out to the part of town where those kind of people lived. It was a section of Belize called Yarborough. And while we were in Yarborough, we were introduced by our friend Sam to John Scorn. It was spelled Scorn but pronounced *Scone*. And we got to know John Scorn.

He was a small dude, black, with a tasty bicycle and a crisp straw hat. John Scorn took his name from his lands like an old European aristocrat. He was John Scorn of Scorn's Bay. His real name was John Burgess. And he looked up his name in the *Oxford English Dictionary* and the listing under Burgess was "the free man of the borough". There he was, John Burgess in Yarborough, and the *Oxford English Dictionary* said he was the free man of the borough.

He became a kind of a nobility. Scorn of Scorn's Bay. He was free. The time the police came to bust him for holding grass, he stood at the door—which was secured only by a screen door hook. John Scorn said,

"Why in the world do you guys come out here because some old white lady in England wants you to come out here and hassle me? I do not understand how this old white lady in England can tell you to do that and you would do that!" He was referring, of course, to the Queen.

The rest of the crew was so abashed that they went away back to the station house for a crowbar to break down the door.

When they came back in some twenty or thirty minutes with a crowbar to break down the door which was only secured with a screen door hook, the house was clean.

John had built his house over the Bay on pilings and said that the Queen's police in their bobby white uniforms and their white fuzzy bobby hats actually had no jurisdiction over John Scorn, who could only be arrested by the harbormaster.

At one point the authorities in British Honduras became so bugged with John Scorn that they shipped him to Jamaica and had him checked out for sanity by the British psychiatrist. The British psychiatrist was completely charmed. A truly original intellect. They sent him back with a clean bill of health. Then John Scorn painted on a four by eight sheet of plywood,

I got my papers to prove I'm sane, Mr. Prime Minister. Where's yours?

I could say more about John Scorn. But he may still live there in Belize. The world has grown small; there is no need to hot up an old friend.

John was a self-made intellect. He hadn't read many books, but he had read them well and through. He had argued every clause of them with his friends. There was always a philosophical or an intellectual discussion going on in the shade under John Scorn's House. True and natural nobility. More truly of the reigning nobilities of the country of British Honduras than the Prime Minister and all his troops.

DET in Boston

T he first time I ever got stoned on something called di-ethyl trypta-mine, a friend of mine and I were dosed with it. It was in Boston, when Margaret and I were coming back up from British Honduras before we went back to San Francisco. I was with this very weird dude who we had picked up in British Honduras, and we were going to come up there and do a light show.

Dave was an M.I.T. whiz kid, who used to win M.I.T.

science fairs and had gotten into M.I.T. as a high school dropout, with a forged high school diploma which he had forged himself. He forged whatever papers he needed to do whatever he wanted to do. He and this Chinese cat were the guys who were the main competitors at the science fairs, who put out the weirdest kind of electronics.

He came back, and I had just pumped him full of light shows. I had just come from San Francisco, and he was hot for it. We were going to do that, and a guy came by to visit. This was a dude who Dave had done a practical joke to. Dave had once put this guy in the bottom of one of the bridge pilings on the Charles River Bridge, a great big square brick thing, hollow on the inside. It took the guy a long time to get somebody to get him out.

So this guy, by way of returning the favor to good old Dave, turned us on to a joint that was heavily laced with di-ethyl tryptamine. Di-ethyl tryptamine lasts a lot longer than DMT and takes about twenty minutes to come on. But it's a similar kind of telepathic trip like di-methyl tryptamine.

I first noticed that something was unusual when I was sitting there thinking,

"Well, the real difference between me and the wall is that the wall is only a four dimensional creature, whereas I actually am a five-dimensional creature..."

Then I thought,

"*You* are *weird*. How did you get this way?" And I began to realize that I was dosed.

The old friend split after he had dosed us, amused at our condition. Then this Chinese guy in black racing leathers showed up. He came in to tell Dave that *he* was going to do the light show trip in this town, and Dave had better back it off.

Dave was getting stoneder and stoneder. At one point, he got up from the discussion and went back into the kitchen. He took a pound box of sugar, and stirred it into a glass of water, as much as he could saturate until it quit dissolving, and drank it, in the hopes that he could bring himself out and be able to *handle* this situation.

He went back into the room, trying to cope, trying to act like he was together, trying to look like he was in the same league as this Chinese dude who was pretty fast and pretty smart, and was coming on pretty strong to him.

Then I watched Dave catch on that he was telepathic. When he caught on, he went on a power trip instantly, and he copped the Chinese guy's mind *without saying a word*. He completely copped his mind by either withholding or giving him reinforcement for things he would say—and the Chinese dude went from something like,

"Well, you haven't got a chance. You may have some good ideas this cat from San Francisco told you, but me and my coolies"—he called the electronics techs who worked for him his coolies—"me and my coolies can outdo you," to where he was saying,

"Well, maybe it would be better if we *didn't* compete—or maybe we could throw our stuff in together." And then he just maybe-maybe-maybe'd right into giving Dave all of his cards and secrets that he was holding close to his chest, telling him everything he was going to do, and getting kind of abject, and into a pleading relationship with Dave, where he's pleading and begging him, and Dave ain't done nothing but sit there and know that he has the power on, to change the guy's mind completely around without doing anything but conditioning him a little bit.

Dave was a hard charger. He's dead now. He went diving after something he'd forgotten while he was down with his tank. He thought he'd just run down without a tank and pick it up. So he stuck a couple of weights in the pockets of his jeans, and hopped over the side. He never came back up.

But he was an amazing dude, who took so much for free from the M.I.T. cafeteria, that his last name became the word for schlepping things out of the cafeteria. He ran a business when he was twelve where he was doing import stuff from other countries. He used letterheads which he had printed up, with pictures of factories with many smoking stacks and stuff. When he was at M.I.T., he worked his way through school by going over to Polaroid and picking up the junk out of their dumpsters, and selling it to Italy, to sunglasses manufacturers. He did some good light show stuff at the Boston Tea Party.

The Boston Tea Party turned out to be a grand success. Later on Dave sent us two pictures, one for me, and one for Margaret. The picture he sent for me was of himself sitting behind the desk with his lap full of money, with the desk covered up full of money, and of somebody walking into the front of his office with his arms loaded full of money. The picture he sent to Margaret was a picture of himself peeing on the back wheel of a bus.

I helped design the Boston Tea Party, and got aced completely out of it when this guy came along who was a lawyer, who had some money to back us up. I watched him and Dave look at each other and say,

"Well, I understand why you, but why *him*?"

Number Fifteen: Broderick Street

We were up in the loft above Broderick Street, a beautiful room. It was a loft where the walls were about four feet high, and slanted in to a flat roof in the middle. It had a single light bulb in the ceiling with a colorful mandala poster draped under it. It had a rusty iron lamp with a piece of parchment for a shade casting a shaft of light straight down onto a big fat easy chair. In front of that easy chair was a six-foot round table, about two feet high, where we rolled joints, cleaned dope, broke kilos, whatnot. Out in the front was a great big picture window with a window seat, and in the back of the room—all one room, except for the kitchen and bathroom—in the back of the room was a mattress over on the floor with a closet, consisting of some clothes hanging on the wall by the bed.

I remember one of the first trips I had with Margaret there. I looked into her mind, and I had my eyes closed. Margaret came inside my mind, and we were together there, inside my mind. It was like long, mirror or ice-sided corridors. Suddenly she manifested herself inside my mind with a cat face, and smiled at me with a cat mouth. I knew I'd always be with her; we'd never really separate, because we were telepathic. It made me want to meet other members of her family. We got really high and really, really telepathic.

I got a flash that I was telepathic with my sister. To find out, I decided to go call her on the telephone. I got downstairs, and I got down to the porch in front. Then I started thinking,

Margaret, come over and look out the window, so I can tell we're still telepathic, even though I'm down here.

And she thought back at me,

Naw, I ain't gonna do it. You wouldn't do well on the affirmation, because you're kind of on a trip.

That was telepathic, clear as a bell.

I got into a telepathic

You come over to this window!

Answered by a telepathic

Uh, unh! No way! I ain't coming!

I couldn't get my sister, but while I was downstairs using the phone, I was called up by a friend of mine, Ken, from writing school. Ken called me up and I started telling him,

"I am stoned. I am telepathic."

"You know, I can feel you. Right now, over this telephone, I can feel you. We are telepathic. I wonder how telepathic we are. Well, if we're *really* telepathic, you can call me back."

And he hung up.

I didn't know his phone number.

We Are All One

here was another time when we
were tripping on Broderick Street,
Margaret was lying on the bed
with a pillow over her head,
being kind of sick or something. Another
guy, Charlie, was completely on his own
trip. It looked like he was in a playpen. You
could look at him and see toys and stuffed
animals.

Well, Charlie's on his own trip, and he has his playpen to keep
him out of the major trip out here while the rest of us get really

seriously high.

A couple of other things like that were going on. We were sitting around the room, and then all of a sudden, everything came into focus and clicked together at once; and we became, everyone in the room, absolutely perfectly telepathic with one another. All of us.

Charlie dropped it and got off his trip.

Margaret sat up and took the pillow off her head.

It was as if a light had been turned on. We were all completely telepathic in our head.

The first things we thought were,

Gratitude, to see it, firsthand, and all of us know it, and know it cold. We did that, for a while. We tried to say something loving or complimentary about people, but it introduced relativity at that place, and somebody thought,

Well, if there's something we can say nice, why don't we say something nice about everybody, or

Did I say something not nice about you? What could I mean that was not nice about you?

Oh, that old thing? Oh. I didn't really mean to bring that up, now.

Well, here it is now.

Don't think that. It's going to make it come apart.

Don't think that!

No, don't!

No, don't think that now. We'll come apart!

We're coming apart. We're going to lose it!

We're losing it. We're losing it!

Aww, shit!

Mind Cop, Magic & Psychology

he Human Be-In took place in a polo field in San Francisco. It was the first time the San Francisco hippies walked out of their apartments, walked out into the middle of that big green grassy polo field, and saw each other all together at once in one place.

As I came up to the Human Be-In, walking from my apartment on Broderick Street, I got several blocks away from the polo field and the energy and vibrations were so strong that I trembled and my knees shook, and my stomach turned to water and I had to sit and lean against a tree and wait a while till I could build up my strength to walk up close to that great gathering.

As I stepped out of the woods up onto the top edge of the polo field I saw a mounted policeman sitting on his horse on the edge of the woods. Someone came up to him and said,

"I've lost something down in that crowd. Help me go down in that crowd."

The mounted policeman said,

"I can't go down in that crowd, lady. All those people are smoking grass."

That was the gathering at which the Hell's Angels became incensed because the power supply for the band became interrupted. They did their first public citizen act—they stood straddling the power line at every joint from the power pole to the edge of the stage. They wanted to be sure the rock 'n' roll was not interrupted again. This was the very meeting when the Grateful Dead got the idea to have the Hell's Angels for the security at Altamont.

At the Human Be-In there was a girl who was stoned on acid, and I walked up and saw this guy looking at her *real* unsmiling, and waving an incense stick in her face and looking to me like he was trying to hypnotize her. I walked up and said,

"This guy looks like he's trying to hypnotize you or intimidate you or something. Are you in need of being rescued?"

And she said, "Yes."

Sometimes you would just see somebody about to do something to somebody's mind or free will while they were really stoned, and you'd try to make it so they didn't have to have some great big old weird gleech in their consciousness where somebody had taken it over for a while or something. I was always into realizing the potentiality for head-cop and retrogression that were possible in acid: its most dangerous side-effect.

Schizophrenia is really like being stoned. Some people call

47

it a psychotomimetic. When you deal with folks who we call schizophrenics, if they are real schizophrenics, many of their experiences will be like acid experiences. You can be more or less telepathic. You can maybe read someone's mind really accurately—or, you can *misread* a whole bunch of cues on them, and apply your own total meaning to the whole thing, and completely misread somebody's mind.

Another thing is that, when you're stoned, you're in the subconscious world. And you see people's subconscious. And somebody who may be a perfectly nice person in the context you're actually meeting them in, for example a doctor in a hospital, might be undergoing a series of fights with his wife, and have a lot of anger bottled up in him from another context; and to someone who is psychotic, he would look not like a doctor, but like an angry person. And for an angry person to be cued in the trappings of power, white clothes, stethoscope, being taken care of by all the nurses who jump at his beck and call, the trappings of power and an angry person lead to one of the commonest hallucinations, which is that you are Trapped in the Hands of the Nazis—*Here I am, man, they got me at last, what can I do? The Nazis have got me!*

A lot of folks who are freaking out in hospitals, people who got taken to hospitals for acid, had real bad trips *after* they got to the hospital, many times, worse than the one they were having before they went.

Much of that was being incompletely telepathic: seeing someone's unconscious motivations, and not realizing that they were telepathic, and assuming those motivations were conscious.

You might have someone who is really horny, and all they think about is getting some here, and getting some there, and how everybody looks and how everybody feels, and trying to get it on with this one or that one—really drawn up with that; and at the same time, they might be a clerk in a police station. They process information, they file information, they do their job; they serve the societal function. And inside, they're just roaring with all that stuff. And you bring in somebody who's on acid,...

I remember one time going down Broderick Street, I saw a naked lady being corralled by a lot of cops. I came and muscled through the cops to the front of the crowd, and got close to her face. She looked at me, and as she looked at me, relief went over her face. She was very glad to see me. She tried to say something, but she couldn't keep her mind together. And she went back to the minds of all the cops who were watching her writhe naked there on the sidewalk. And she began reacting to them louder than she could react to anything else, and she started screaming,

"Lay me! Lay me! Lay me, please!" and lay on her back.

They picked her up and threw her in the squad car. She climbed up in the back seat, and tried to expose herself out the back window of the car. They took her away. And in her sensitive state, she was being driven by their desires. And she was going to be written down for every thing that she did, which was an expression of the minds of her captors. She was going to have to go to some mental institution and explain to some psychiatrist why she did that. She did that because she was peaking on a heavy psychedelic, and she was being mistreated by the police. They were more interested in her naked body than they were in protecting her naked mind.

Folks who are schizophrenic meet with all those doctors, and all those orderlies, and all those cleaning people and all. Those folks are like ordinary folks, a lot of them. And some of the schizophrenics that come in are very telepathic, and picking up stuff from all those people.

Sometimes folks came from out of town into San Francisco like a meteor with a bright flash on their entrance and a quick crash. Ol' Nashville Jim—good looking young dude. He tried to convince you he was from nice folks. He said,

"My family's gone to college. Many of them have been in

49

the military."

He was trying to let me know that he considered himself to be nice folks.

He would come to me and ask me questions. I watched him go and mix up with Haight Street. And he began to move with a weird tribe that was known as speed dealers. As he went out with these speed dealers, he began to get stranger and stranger.

One time I was walking out on Haight Street and found Nashville Jim squatted down on the sidewalk behind a little square hole in the cement where a young tree was struggling to grow. Playing with the dried dog turds and sifting them through his fingers like they was jewels. I stopped and said,

"Jim! What are you on?"

He turned to me and leered, and said in a voice reeking with ego,

"Just the best there is, that's all."

I was a little slowed down by that. I walked around to the opposite side of the block where the health food store was, to buy a few health foods, and thought, *I can't leave that young guy in that kind of condition.* So we fired up the truck and drove back around the block to pick him up. We were just a minute too late: the police were just loading him into a paddy wagon and taking him off down to the Park Street Station.

Then there are the ones who, because they're telepathic, think they're going to cop your mind. You can hardly deal with them, because they're so busy trying to cop your mind. They're just right in your face trying to cop your mind all the time, and everything they say is suspect and untrustworthy, and has to be inspected to see why did they say it. And that is how they receive your communication, too: that everything you say is so untrustworthy that they can't believe it. You can't say anything hypothetical or arguable to someone like that. You have to say stuff that's self-evident, and really true, or they won't listen.

The whole catalog of craziness, like Adler's ideas of ego-dominance and stuff, was exposed by acid. There was such a thing as people who were into ego-dominance. That was all they cared about was whether they dominated you. That was what their hobby was, and that was what they worked toward. There was something that I had said to me two or three times when I ran into someone like that and got checkmated, skunnered, or whatever. When they would stick it to me, they would say,

"I'm sure you understand." They mean,

It's what you would do to me if you had me in that place.

The other areas that were explored by Jung, the collective unconscious and the relationship of dreams and reality, synchronicity and all that kind of stuff, are just raging, boiling, roaring through the acid world, all that kind of thing.

Dr. David Smith, of the Haight Street Free Clinic said,

"Acid lowers your powers of discrimination until everything seems important." When I heard that, I said,

"No. Acid *raises* your powers of *integration* until everything *is* important."

Acid was giving you ego deaths. And ego deaths were almost like real deaths; so we had a mythology of the ego death that went on. That's why the Grateful Dead poster came out with the skeleton and the roses on it. It was ego death and rebirth, life growing from the bones. It was ego death and rebirth—lovely to get to do it. Sometimes it was really graceful, and sometimes it was really...

One time we had been tripping along in the early tripping things where you see colors and stuff like that, and suddenly it came, as clear as a knock on the door, that this was *it,* and here we went. *We began to run down.* The lights went down from white to yellow to dark orange. We'd get down, and we'd almost be completely run down, and at some waayyy-back-there level of my mind, I would understand that we were not all going to land together, and that it would be better if we all landed together. And we would go back up a little ways, like lifting a helicopter up. We'd back up a little ways, and we'd adjust a little bit, until we were all going to touch down exactly together.

One lady who was present looked me in the eyes, very plain, and says,

"Is there anything you can do about this?"

And I said,

"No. There ain't *anything* I can do about this."

She said,

"Okay," and composed herself.

We took it down one more time, and we lit on the bottom all together, and stopped.

We lay there empty for a while and then we came back to life, and came back up, and floated back up through the planes to where there was lights and everything was back to normal, more or less.

That part of me that was back in there bringing us up and down and making us all land together at once was a very interesting part, and I never forgot it. I thought,

Look at that. As wiped out as that, as down the karmic chute as that, as committed as that, and still something in there has control, and observes, and makes judgments, like a good pilot flying by the seat of his pants.

I've had highly structured original poetry pressed out of my mouth so fast that it was like a chain being pulled out of my mouth, and my lips had to hurry to open and close over the links as they were pulled from me—and put out straight poetry, highly structured, as fast as I could possibly move my mouth—as an accent, just as easy as assuming a funny walk.

I've done superstitious things, too. I've accidentally raised a bad vibe, and done something symbolic to lay that vibe to rest, and then clung to that symbol for a long time. I wore a nice set of scarabs around my neck for a while because they were very magicky, and I had had this interesting trip.

I was actually toying with the Manichaean heresy, which

is the idea that it's a contest between God and the devil, and that the outcome is somehow uncertain. I was postulating that there was an evil intelligence. I gave it a nickname. I called it Mordor, Incorporated. As in Mordor from the Trilogy, and Murder, Incorporated. And the vibe was so true to the thing that I meant while I was talking about that, that I evoked that, and left us feeling weird. So I said,

"I need a talisman." I used to make up magic out of whole cloth, and this seemed like an occasion that called for it.

"I need a talisman, to lay this vibe." And I went rustling around through stuff, knowing that I would know it when I found it. As I ruffled around, I came upon this exquisite scarab necklace that Margaret's girlfriend in high school had stolen from her mother and given to Margaret. It was old, with antique ceramic scarabs and a chain. When I looked at it, it had a winged scarab flying off into the sun, dragging another scarab behind it on a link. And the symbology of it meant to me that those who figure it out are not going to leave those who don't figure it out, that we are all going to stick together. It was a Bodhisattvic image to me, and it had a lot of power and beauty to it, and the object psychically glowed as I thought that stuff. It seemed shiny to me, and had a good clean vibe, and reminded me of a clean idea and a clean thing. And I said,

"We'll just take this." And I put it on, and it seemed to dispel the chill that I had brought with my careless evocation of something grim at a high, stoned place.

It reminded me of that, and I wore it for a long time. But then I remembered, somewhere along the line, that I couldn't take sides that way, because that was the side of the Pharoah, after all, and I was more like one of the Jews.

For a time, I wore a bunch of magic on me. I wore a cross, and a Star of David, and a fish made out of silver, and a yang and yin, and maybe a marijuana leaf—a variety of stuff, trying to indicate, in magical language, the direction I went in. Some folks liked it better than others. Some folks didn't like to see a cross hanging amidst a bunch of other symbols. I wore a flag for a while, a great big old rhinestone and silver flag. It sparkled. I gave it up because somebody got stuck by it while hugging me.

The silver fish, I understood some of the strange mythology of *In Watermelon Sugar*. I knew Brautigan slightly, and I felt the acid weird in his books, and I wore that silver fish. A lot of people did. It was a small cult. I was a member of several minor cults, and some large ones. I had a Blue Camel Bead, thought to dispel the Evil Eye.

But there was some stuff I could not do, or hack. Like the time fifteen hundred hippies pulled Bhaktivedanta on a juggernaut with seven-foot high wheels with a purple canopy on it down through the Golden Gate Park on the ends of long ropes, strewing flowers in his path while they dragged him on down through the park. Could not hack it.

I always, in my heart of hearts at the time, felt that the people who joined Hare Krishna, and frequently those who became Jesus freaks and those kinds of moves, from the position of being a tripping hippy, did it because they scared themselves somehow, and they were going to a refuge. They were not going towards a thought-out move, and they were not going towards an enlightenment; they were running from something because they were afraid. Many of those who joined those movements, who later on said, "What am I doing here?" and drifted on out of them, did that because their fear of acid had died down enough that they could resume normal life.

Acid terrified many people. Acid terrified me many times. I have not the slightest doubt that acid could terrify me again. Not the slightest doubt. But somehow, I don't seem to be afraid of that. It doesn't bother me at all.

Tripping well on acid was like being an athlete. It took tremendous amounts of courage. And you had to rely more on your innate character than on how smart you might think you were. Stuff would come on you so fast that you would not be thinking it linearly while you were reacting to it; you'd be reacting so fast to it that you'd be on to your reflexes. If you had pretty good habits, you'd tend to rise. If you didn't have good habits, you'd tend not to.

The thing about getting up and looking for a talisman is just recognizing that when you're in a position where the vibes are going in a way that you don't like, you are not bound to vibratory means alone to change the result. You can up and start doing things in the material plane which are going to have results. You just don't lay back and let something happen to you and try to vibe it not to happen while it runs over you. You get up and start taking *action*. And those folks who take action are the high survivors.

We knew a young guy who was an intelligent young guy, but his problem was that he was the one follower of a King and Creator of the Universe who lived down in Brisbane. And between them, they wrote communiques to send to heads of state. They gave each other *full* ruffles and flourishes. I met that guy again years later and said,

"Oh yeah, you were the guy who was with that guy in Brisbane, aren't you?"

And I saw him regret it. I saw him think, *Aw, nuts. Here's a nice guy who I'd like to meet, and he identifies me with that dingaling I used to be with back in Brisbane. Aw, nuts. It sure did mess my reputation up bad.*

One of the easiest crazies is to go into a Godlike viewpoint, and come out the other side and be attached to it, and not want to give it up, to try to hang on to it after you've passed over the peak of it. You would get folks like that who would try to pull omens out of the environment to try to prove *everything*. When you get into freelance omenizing, you can self-justify everything that you want to do by the omens that happen to you.

I have a view of omens. I was riding down the connecting highway from Highway One over to Ben Lomond in my old, slow, Metro truck one time. I came across a sign that said,

Danger. Buried Pipeline. As I looked at the sign, the *Danger* on it jumped out at me so hard, and attracted my attention so strong and grabbed my consciousness so hard when I saw it, that I immediately pulled over to the side of the road and stopped. It was raining slightly. And as I pulled over to the side of the road, a car came by from behind us making eighty or ninety miles an hour, *sscheeww!* past us. He didn't even start hitting the brakes for the next corner until he was several hundred yards past us. He came past us and he still had his foot in it. If we'd been out there where we had been a second or so before that, we would have been right in his path.

In my model of telepathy, something like that is the intelligence of the receiving set to take a raw vibration and translate it into a piece of information. And to do this, it frequently has to be ricocheted off the environment. It feels to me like the higher intellect chooses those parts of the environment which carry the meaningful messages, and amplifies them so they reflect back into the sensorium, where they can then be read as the omens. And it doesn't require a lot of superstition to make it work. Some of that stuff comes in and you say,

"Oh, that's a good one. I like that one," and another one comes in and you say,

"Oh, that's a good one, too. I like that one, too."

You can follow a bunch of those like that, and you can find yourself on some sort of train that leads to something obsessive and compulsive, something which you can't quit thinking about, and part of your mind tells you, *If you don't quit thinking about this, you're liable to go do it.* And the part that thinks, *Oh, my God, If I don't quit thinking about this I'm going to do it, and I can't quit thinking about doing this . . .*

When I talk about crazy as my backyard, I mean that these are places I have been, or I wouldn't know them this well. They are places I have survived, they are like mega-emotions I have experienced, although any one of them, if taken uncritically and solidly, would be a sufficient load of craziness to squash you.

Some people think there's a real world, where everything is real, and a magic world, where everything is magic. But the thing about the magic world is that, in the magic world, some stuff is real and some ain't. That's just how the magic world is. And if you're going to deal in the magic world, that's the stuff you have to deal in. Of course, the straightforward way to deal with the magic world is to ask, out loud, in front of everyone, for things which are good for everyone: to pray.

Many times I saw folks try to move stuff with their head. And one time I think I saw it done. But I also remember very clearly trying to hoke it, trying to fake it, pushing it, starting it swinging it a little bit and see if that would get it going. That's the thing about psychic phenomena on the material plane. We were all having *outrageous* experiences astrally. And the edge of doubt in the psychedelic world is when you demand your material-plane proof. So that question of material-plane proof kept coming up.

One night, Paul and I were on acid. Margaret and John and someone else, I believe, were not. Paul and I were sitting at a table, and we had read in a science fiction book about balancing a cigarette paper on a pin stuck through a matchbook. So we stuck a pin through a matchbook and we balanced a paper on it. We sat around it, and looked at it, and tried to think at it and stuff.

And Paul, all of a sudden, said.

"I've *got* it!"

And as he said it, the paper started moving. Not just moving, but moving pretty sprightly, and apparently dancing to the music on the radio. Nice and in time with it.

Of course the mind has the ability to integrate all that sort of thing, except *why was it moving anyway?*

Margaret saw it move. Everybody saw it move. Paul said he could do it. And it looked like he did it.

57

I have that memory very firmly in my mind. Every time I remember that memory, since it originally happened, I look at it, and I've bit it like a gold coin, to see if it was real. And it's one of the realest memories I have back in there, is watching that paper dance. I don't know what to say about that, except that's one thing I saw, once.

I went through a lot of changes with him. We did telepathic manifestations. Paul and John and I and a couple of other friends did telepathic manifestations around among one another, that were like playing catch with a ball.

One time I was sitting on the bed under the light, and Paul was sitting on the other side of the room on the window seat, twenty-five feet away or so, and he was trying to attract my attention telepathically, but was not having any luck.

And then, all of a sudden, I was *struck* with something that knocked me flat on the bed, **Whomp!!**

I came bouncing up and said,

"What was **that?!?**"

And Paul said,

"That was me."

And I said,

"What in the *world* did you do?"

He said,

"Well, I was trying to attract your attention, and I wasn't having any luck. So I thought I would take a concept and rev it up real strong, and see if I could create a strong concept and then throw that at you. So I took the idea of Thor's hammer spinning, and spun it until it was just a fast blur in my mind, and then threw it at you."

It *flattened* me on the bed, just like a physical blow.

We had a lot of weird stuff go down among us that made us think that this was a malleable medium we were moving around in. There was no question to *us* that magic was real. There were ground rules for magic, and if you pursued it a little bit it was at least ethics; and if you pursued it far

58

enough; it was religion.

Paul showed me other things, too. We had a game we would play sometimes. He could just sit there and *rev*, like revving up an engine, and turn up the color. He would sometimes grit his teeth and look serious, and sometimes he would look angelic and beautiful. I'd look at him and say,

"Aw, you look like an old stained-glass window. You look like an old medieval Archbishop or something. Look at him rev."

And he would turn it up, and I would give that kind of feedback to him, and he would rev.

We had a very close relationship, psychically and telepathically. I think he's an unfinished relationship. I have a lot of unfinished relationships from back when we were moving so fast that if somebody stepped out of bounds, you couldn't stop and go hunt them up. You had to stay and keep going. But I really loved him, and we spent a lot of time together in a really close, stoned relationship. We tripped together maybe fifty times. Many times I would get up from the previous evening's party, and I would clean the house in the morning, and go sit in the window and wait for him to come. When he showed up we would turn on to the first joint of the day together, and get stoneder and stoneder during the day. Sometimes we would drop acid and sit at opposite ends of the window seat, propped up, and just look in each other's eyes and let it roll. Very stoned. We had some good trips together.

He was a natural driver of anything. One of our friends had a little English car that really handled well, a Morris or something like that. He would drive that, and he would *slide* sideways, come around corners bouncing until you could see daylight under all four wheels, sliding around corners, under perfect control, with perfect good humor, a composed smile and enjoying himself. And he was graceful to trip with.

One night he borrowed my motorcycle, and was out on acid on my motorcycle on Mount Tam in the middle of the night, driving around. He was incredibly coordinated. He's the only gringo I know who could easily do a Scorpion, for instance, which is where you kip up and balance on your forearms, and let your feet dangle down from the top and touch you on the top of your head.

In the middle of the night, I woke up and I saw the handlebars and the speedometer, and a patch of illuminated road in front of me for a second, very clearly. Very clear.

Rockin' Jody Morningstar

ockin' Jody was a grass smoker at San Francisco State College, and I was a grass smoker. We had a long friendship. I saw him go through many changes. I saw him with pretty rich parents, expensive-clothes kind of place; I saw him go away to New Mexico and come back barefoot in robes, wild-eyed and crazy looking, with his hair like a great curly blond halo around his head, and weird looking. And then I saw him try to fetch himself back into Florsheim shoes and button-down collar shirts again.

Sometimes he was strung out on speed, and when he was, the thing that made him different from the other speed freaks was just that he had rich parents, and he never did gutter-out bottom, although he was doing a lot of speed. Sometimes he wasn't doing speed, and he was doing a lot of acid.

I would hang out with him because he was fun, he was telepathic; he was interesting.

We had this agreement that it was the church. Not *a* church. *The* church. It didn't belong to nobody. It was everybody's. Those folks who had visions of it was who got to know about it; and if you didn't have visions of it, you didn't know about it.

We felt it was a church meeting *every time* good friends and good people got together and really got high and loved each other and went into being telepathic and high with one another; and we tried to be that way about it.

It was funny, because he was so expedient on one hand; but he was real about stuff. He ran in a heavy rip-off atmosphere, and had a very strong technology for surviving; and I learned a lot of my survival technology from him, because he was trying to rip me off.

Sometimes he was dishonest . . . and sometimes he was just startlingly truthful. I think he was one of the first people I ever heard speak truthfully about religion, and say that he believed in God—and have a sincere ring of truth in his voice, like he really meant it. And that kind of caught me. I'd heard a lot of *hare* this and mumbo-jumbo that, but . . .

We knew that if you were in the middle of a deep bummer, that you could appeal for good vibes and for help—and there was such a thing, and it was there. Whether it came out of the woodwork, or came down from Heaven like a lightning bolt, or came up through you like the Hulk, it was there.

He always had a lot of fancy stuff around. A fancy buck

knife you could hammer through a bolt; or a Winchester octagon barrel 25/35 museum piece deer rifle; he had beautiful Indian artifacts sometimes.

One of his artifacts was a beautiful peyote gourd, with nice beadwork on the side of it. When he went to Arizona one time, he brought his peyote gourd to a peyote meeting with some of the local Indians around Gallup.

During the course of the meeting, one of the chiefs, a medicine chief, looked over at Rockin' Jody's gourd, which he was rattling, and said,

"*You* ain't a road chief. *You* can't have a gourd like that," and snatched the gourd out of his hand, and took it and kept it—and sent Rockin' Jody back to San Francisco without his gourd.

Rockin' Jody was a student. He was taking some comparative religion courses, which is where he learned some of the ceremonial stuff; but he was taking some other kind of major, and he did his homework and he graduated and went and took a job in that field. I don't even know if he trips any more.

He did funny things to me.

I went into the Family Dog one time. I looked over, and there was a piece of equipment draped with the blue field of an American flag. It was part of Owsley's equipment. The stars on it were all upside down, and I didn't like it that way. I liked it better with the stars all right side up. So I went over and just turned this piece of stuff over, thinking,

Well, I don't know if that's going to have any magical effect on him or not, but *I* felt better about it.

I saw Jody in the crowd at the boogie later that evening, and I said,

"Hey, I turned old Owsley's equipment cover around the other way. I turned it to right side up."

And he started hollering at me, real loud, in front of all these people, real sarcastic,

"Oh, *Stephen*! Oh, you're so *magical*! *Wow!*"

There was this lady I loved pretty good. She was a funny, elfin thing. I saw her shoot a large rainbow out of her head one time. She had mysterious dancing eyes, and she was a turn-on and very sexy. She had a sports car and she drove it fast, and she was good, and she didn't have wrecks. I really loved her. I tripped with her quite a bit.

One day I was visiting with her, and we stopped over at Rockin' Jody's. One thing that happened with Rockin' Jody was that he would have some just killer weed, and would stone me, and then do some kind of mini-number on my head while I was peaking on some kind of strange boo that he always seemed to be in the flow of. If a kilo came into town, he got half a lid.

We began smoking this grass. I don't know how bad I was tripping, but enough that it was obvious to Jody that I was tripping some. All of a sudden, he sat up straight and looked at me very severely. And he seemed to get very stoned and very heavy-looking to me, until he looked sort of teacherish. And he said,

"I see a sort of red aura around you that indicates a lot of spiritual pride. You ought to reduce it."

I stopped to digest that because I was serious. I was trying to get stoned. I took stuff seriously. I had just smoked a bunch of good grass, and got this thrown in my lap.

We were all sitting in a circle, Rockin' Jody and this lady and I, crosslegged. While I was still trying to get it together, Jody spun around on his bottom so instead of his knee pointing towards the center of the circle, his head was. He lay down on his back, and laid his head in her lap. And she leaned forward over him and kissed him a long, heavy kiss.

I sat there, and my mind just blew, and blew, and blew. Before my very eyes, an agreement was made that such a thing could go down in front of me like that, and it just made me know that I was not seeing all the levels. There must have been a modicum of truth in what he said, because something went down that I just didn't see. I almost wanted them to run that one by me, again. I just didn't know how he could do that.

I learned about that later on, too. I saw that it's easy for a person to be on enough of a trip that everyone can know they're on a trip, and make agreements to do numbers to them to blow their mind, without them even noticing or catching on. But when I understood that that was being done to me, that Jody and this lady were doing that to me, it was a real teaching. *Bang!*

That's a rough kind of psychiatry. It certainly avoids the pitfalls of transference.

Rockin' Jody was very competitive. He messed with me for a while before I even realized he was messing with me. Over a years-long relationship, I realized he was messing with me.

When I did realize it, my first reaction was not to get outraged or run or anything. I thought, *Oh! This is the name of the game, and these are the ground rules. All right. Batter up. Let's roll, now that we know what the game is.* So then we began playing the game, and we went through some changes.

Rockin' Jody had incredible chutzpah, if anything he ever said was to be believed, which some of it must have been. One time he was having a paranoid bummer while driving a rented Mustang with a U-Haul trailer full of kilos up from Tijuana on the freeway, and was stopped by the cops. And he survived these things, somehow. Sometimes the way he survives them, is he goes real cool, and just stays real cool until he gets out of the situation. And sometimes, he just weirds out until he gets out from being weird, somehow.

He would tell me these stories about the weird things he had done that would just nag on the edge of my conscience. And I would say,

"*What* are you telling me?"

It sounded like he had seriously copped somebody's mind in effect, just taken them over for a time. *And there were a couple of times when he seemed to be trying very hard to do that to me.* But he was fine company. He was great to smoke dope with.

He lived in a world where that kind of thing went on. Sometimes he was copping other people's heads; and sometimes they were copping his.

He would go through phases like that. It was obvious to me that he was experiencing the same kinds of things that I was. He was a little ahead of me in class, though. He was a little more into it than I was for a while, until I got to the level where it was no longer a matter of who was farther into it, but rather it was a question of whether I was going to come out of this owning my own gourd and in free possession of myself, or was I going to come out of this being owned by somebody?

I began to teach, out loud, that there was such a thing as head cop, and that you could get your head copped, and that you ought to be sure you weren't getting your head copped, and that you ought to know what the symptoms of head cop were. See your dentist twice a year and brush every day, about head cop. I tried to teach a little head-cop prophylaxis in the scene. Some of my earliest stuff was on account of seeing the astounding potential, not just for institutional, but for personal mind control. And I realized that this was the real level of magic, and that people who were dishonest at this level were who the real black magicians were. I learned that there was such a thing as black magic. If somebody cops your head so bad that they send you on another whole chain of life that leads you down a lot of bad things and ruins your potential and you don't ever recover, they've got your soul. Copped your head and got your soul.

I came to the end of my relationship with Rockin' Jody pretty much about the same time I got my Metro truck. Before that time, my personal life didn't count very much; so I dealt a few lids to make it, even dealt a few caps of acid and stuff. But I came to a place where I could no longer pass money over dope. I had to give up that entire aspect of it. I

realized that the relationship I had been having with Rockin'
Jody *had* been a bit of a head-cop, which I discovered when I
started telling him I wanted to quit doing it. He got *most*
uptight. Me and Margaret finally had to...I had some acid
and I had some money, so I gave him his acid and I gave him
his money, and he said,

"Don't you want to keep a couple of tabs to get high?"
I said,

"I *am* high. Ain't nothing you could give me that could *get*
me high. *Am high now.*"

The last time I saw him he was in a suit, about to leave
San Francisco State College. He stepped into our bus with
us. We were all freaked out hippies, he was in short hair and
a suit. He smoked a joint with us, and as we smoked a joint
together, he did just the faintest little suggestion of the
dance he used to do when he was working strong. When
he'd dance around and talk about what kind of dope it was,
and talk funny with his voice all tight like he was holding a
toke. He just did a little sketch of that dance, and the
thought came to my mind while he was doing it,

A shadow of his former self.

Rotten Button Tea

he peyote meeting is sometimes sort of a competitive rip-off medium. Any psychedelic teaching is sometimes a competitive rip-off medium, I believe. At least with the guys I tripped with, who were outlaws anyway.

One time Rockin' Jody and I were going to have a peyote meeting out in Stinson Beach. On the way over to the meeting, we stopped by a place to pick up some stuff. Then, on the way out as we walked away, Rockin' Jody picked up a bundle of firewood and carried it over to the car.

"Did you pay for that?" I asked.

"Sure," he said.

"You couldn't have," I said. "You didn't have time. Man, go back and *pay* for that. Where are you *at*?"

"Well, you don't understand, " he said. "It ain't nothing to rip off the man—it's all part of the Establishment."

"You go back and pay for that!"

So he went back, and he went inside, and was gone inside for a while, and came back out and picked up another bundle of wood, and came on back to the car. He said,

"I got two bundles while I was at it."

We drove on over to the house. The peyote we had was some that had been in a gunny sack; it was starting to go, and had been thrown in a freezer to stop it from going all the way. We were boiling the entire bottom of this sack.

It was awful tea. It was real bad tea. It made me barf right away—but it also got me *high*.

We went in, and there was a lady who used to sing with the Charlatans in Virginia City, Nevada. She used to sing,

"I got to beat the devil just to satisfy my man,"

Her old man was there, whose tripping name was Travis T. Hip. Travesty. He was the Fire Chief. He got sick, barfed, and fell asleep.

I barfed, and the meeting wasn't going too well. I was lying down, and almost spacing clear out, when Rockin' Jody said,

"At *least* you could eat enough peyote to keep you *awake!*"

Everybody was trying to play the drum when it got their turn, and sing a song; and nobody could get it up very good. It was like a hard, hard time.

There was this weirdly dressed dude from Texas, dressed really bizarrely, and this cat started coming on kind of black-magicky, and Rockin' Jody said,

"Hey man, you can't come on like that at a peyote meeting."

And this guy says,

"I've been to peyote meetings down in Laredo."

And Jody says,

"You just can't come *on* at a peyote meeting like that, man, you got to come right down the Santa Fe."

The Santa Fe Trail had great significance in the legend.

And this cat straightened up.

Jody was running the meeting; and as he would direct attention to various parts of his peyote gear spread out on the floor, I would *zap* it with such a jolt as to cause it to just *leap* into consciousness and luminesce.

The fire went out. It didn't make any coals. The fire went away, and just left little ashes in the fireplace. That's when I knew that Rockin' Jody had stolen *both* bundles.

We had made a beautiful peyote road. We had brought in a four-by-eight sheet of plywood, and set it down in front of the fireplace, and brought in a bunch of sand from the beach. We made a beautiful peyote road, six feet across the horns or so. It was a little hill in a half-moon shape, raised up in the middle kind of like a freeway ramp raises up, comes to a little peak, and then back down at the ends. Rockin' Jody said that the shape of the peyote road shows that a man comes from the earth and rises to a small eminence, and returns to the earth again. That was the kind of stuff he would say sometimes.

I made the peyote road, and he gave me a big, beautiful eagle feather, four inches wide and a foot long. I smoothed the peyote road with the feather, sculpting the sand into a perfect shape. I really tried hard.

But that's not where we were at in the middle of the night. In the middle of the night, it was puking and sick and bad feelings and arguing and complaining, and the fire going out.

I went out and barfed, and when I came back in, Rockin' Jody gave me another one of those kind of lessons that he used to give me, sometimes, out of nowhere.

70

He came over to me. He looked at me like *he did not know me*. He was the Road Chief of this meeting, and he was going to do what was right; it didn't matter whether he knew me or not. He looked at me and said,

"This guy's been sick. Cedar him off before he can come in."

The fire was still going then. They fired it up a little bit, and threw a bunch of cedar on it to smoke. They got a turkey-wing fan, and got little balls of smoke off the fire, and chivvied them across the room with the fan, and hit me with the little balls of smoke, and powdered them down all over me with the turkey wing fan, and put cedar wood smoke all over me, to purify me from having been sick.

With all of that, that pretty road and trying to do it that way, . . .

Rockin' Jody kept his peyote down—I have never *seen* anybody fight *so hard* to avoid barfing. He would just be *hit* with these giant convulsions that he would just *stop*, either at his throat or at his lips, and hold it. And if it got into his mouth, he would re-swallow it, and hang right on to it. He was *not* going to barf. He was *very* strong, and *very* proud.

Along in through here, with nobody having a good time, Rockin' Jody realized that what we were really ready for was for this sucker to be over. And it gave him an idea for a song. He started singing the song, and it was true enough that the other people could tap their feet to it. He sang,

Peyote church is a feel-good-in-the-morning church.
Peyote church is a feel-good-in-the-morning church.
Drum and sing all night, and gonna feel good in the morning.
Peyote church is a feel-good-in-the-morning church.

We sang along like that, and rode down the long, tough hours from like three or four in the morning on into daylight, chanting and singing together, praying for the sun to come up, waiting for the light at the end of the tunnel.

And when the sun came up, we *were* happy; and we *did*

have a good time. And it was stoned.

Even the worst kind of peyote meeting has a value and a utility.

Morning with White Indian Blanket Sunrise

 remember coming to my senses in the morning, sitting with the sun streaming over me, with a white hand-woven Indian blanket with gold trim at the ends, and some feathers and some beads and stuff on me, some Indian stuff, and everybody treating me *real good* for a while.

Then that kind of fades, and I don't remember how I got into it, and I don't remember how I got out of it. But at some point in this trip, I got jacked up and ceremonied on by my friend, Rockin' Jody, and that was the result of it.

I had a couple of trips like that with him and a bunch of eagle feathers. He kept coming up with gicondous eagle feathers, about a foot long and four inches wide, and when you moved them they tried to fly in your hand. They had what felt like magical properties to me. When I was stoned on acid, I felt like I could draw lines in space and I could open doors. At one point I took two feathers and held them together, and then started to spread them apart. And as they got farther and farther apart, they got harder and harder to pull. When I had them two or three feet apart, it was the limit of my strength to be able to hold them apart; but *between them could be seen a vision.* I thought so, anyway. That's what I was trying to do.

I guess I was a little out there, because Rockin' Jody was on his knees, wondering where I was at, and praying for me.

"Lord, help this man. Lord, he's basically a good man. Please try and help him, Lord."

Charlie and the Drogstore Cafe

ne fine morning I got up and took acid at sunrise. I thought *Well, I'll just drop this acid, and take a bath while it's coming on, and get dressed and go trip somewhere.* So I dropped this acid, a White Lightning, ran a bath, jumped into the bathtub, and became really nauseous in the bathtub. I crawled out of the tub on my hands and knees, rushing so hard I couldn't stand up. I tried to get dressed, flopped around the bathroom for a while, barfed, crawled out into the bedroom,

and had to lay and pant for a long time before I could even try to find clothes or anything. Immediately roaring off the line, the way you did off of White Lightning. After a while, I got it together and decided to go down to Haight Street and have breakfast at the Drogstore Cafe. So we went down and we got into this old powder-blue '50 Ford.

It was funny. When we came back from Boston, we were totally broke. Everything was going wrong. We were being ripped off, and we were even fighting between us. When we got back to the City, the nicest apartment in San Francisco, as far as I was concerned, an illegal fifth floor pad, was open for rent at about sixty-five bucks. A friend of mine happened to have a 1950 powder blue Ford convertible, which he loaned me to use. An old girlfriend laid a pound on me, to break down into lids. And suddenly there I was, completely set up and established.

The 1950 Ford was a bouncy, floaty thing, anyway. I was pretty banged, and my reactions were so hyper-fast that the long, slow loops of that Ford started making me seasick. I had to sit very carefully and quietly and steer very right-down-the-line, because I was really wrecked. We got down there, and I was so *grateful* to get it parked, and not to have to be responsible for a bunch of thing like that, that I actually felt pretty good out on my feet after that.

We were down on Haight Street, early in the morning. A lot of places were closed; a few speed freaks were still up early from the night before. We dropped into the Drogstore Cafe, which was *mostly* speedfreaks still up from the night before. We sat down, and the place was bright, and had big windows. The sun was coming in, but it was weird, anyway, a little bit. It had paisley table covers; but the background between the paisleys was black, and the colors were sort of jangly—electric orange and yellows and stuff that looked pretty funny against the black. I looked over, and the cashier had a very funny look.

It's black and purple and lavender and green, a lot of

funny colors to be stuck together; it looks kind of oil-slicky and not good colors. The guy at the cash register was mad. He had jaw plates of ridged muscles that were almost the same weird colors as the table tops. He was snapping at the other help and the customers. I was tripping a little strangely anyway, from the amount of energy I had to give up to navigate that Ford and get it parked. And this guy came in and saw that I was tripping a little strangely, and wanted to help me out. He was a bit of a sleazy looking dude; he was a little fat, and had short hair, and was wearing a tee shirt and some square pants, and looked more like a bum than a hippy, but he talked the most incredible string of highly intelligent hippy dope talk as he went along, rattling off, "How can there be a dharma when there is no dharma, and if there is no dharma, what is the dharma?" and those kinds of things, which he liked to flash around. His name was Charlie.

Charlie had been a lot of things, some of which he was faintly ashamed of. He saw me looking at the guy behind the cash register, and said,

"Don't mind him, man," and he started telling me this stuff with a sorrowful face and a funny subtle plane. He delivered very funny mixed messages of pain and under-standing and humor that were so funny and essentially good-natured, although based in kind of a weird thing, that it began to lift my spirits and get me high. I dug him a bunch, and he talked about nice concepts.

He laid the concept on me that if you have a piece of paper and you draw a line down the middle of it, it does not make two pieces of paper. And just because something is separated by a surface does not mean it is two things any more than when something is separated by a line. And essentially, the surface of him touched the surface of the medium that existed between me and him, and I touched that medium on the other side, and we touched each other through it; and he was conscious of that.

He was smart and psychedelic and telepathic, but he had a

weird sort of conditioning on him from some strange places he talked about where he had tripped.

He said somebody there had unlimited acid, and there were some folks who seemed to live there full time, and there were others who just passed through and crashed there. He said sometimes people would come through with acid and say, "Open your mouth," and throw some acid in your mouth, and you might get hit more than once a day. He said,

"Sometimes it got so much that I just had to sit down for a while and let it all rush over me. Most of the time, we just tripped around the house. But sometimes the oddest stuff would happen.

"We'd go out, and we'd catch some old conventioner out on the street out by North Beach, or down by Union Square, and we'd bring him home and dose him on acid. When he was peaking pretty good, we'd dance around him and talk about the military-industrial complex, and where it was at to be a businessman, and where it was at for him to be like that, and how about his karma, and try to guide him on an assisted ego death."

Charlie had these funny feelings, like he had been used in some ways. He was an artist, and he drew pictures. He drew a picture that scared me half to death when I finally ever looked at it for real. It was just a picture of a face, kind of stylized. Grecian, a little. And the eyes had pupils in the center, and then blacks, instead of whites. And where the veins and things would have been were white tubes floating in that black void, in non-comprehender perspectives that broke the eyes loose from the face and made them seem to expand alone, those black holes. And they looked out with anguish and anger. They were frightened eyes, they were afraid eyes. I walked by, stoned on acid on another trip, and looked up at the picture on the wall that Charlie had given me. I looked at it, and said,

"Somebody, please come and take this down for me." I

didn't even want to walk up close enough to it to unpin it from the wall, it was so bad.

But I brought Charlie home that morning, and Charlie was kind of a groove in many ways, an intelligent dude. Then he told me about some of his weirder trips, where he had been dosed so many times over at that house. One time he told me about, he decided that space was filled with worms about three inches thick that were invisible, but space was totally filled with them, just sliding around against each other like a bucketful of maggots. These worms were crawling all around him, and he had to talk with his teeth clenched because if he opened his mouth in a big enough opening, a worm would slide inside him, and he had to be very careful that the space worms didn't slide inside him. That was an interesting trip.

Father Christos at the Straight Theater

e had been tripping over at the illegal fifth floor apartment on Broderick Street, me and Paul and David, maybe Charlie and Linda, and we were going to go over to see Father Christos at the Straight Theater. We thought we should do that because the bill had Father Christos back to back with Kenneth Anger at eight o'clock on Sunday morning, and it looked like the sort of thing that we ought to go to, and be of help. So we went there, and we be'd of help in the way that you do.

Things went down on the way that were strange. On the way there, we stopped through the Tea Garden in Golden Gate Park. As we came walking along, on White Lightning and Purple Haze double domes, Owsley's first purple double domes, somebody walked up and said,

"You guys have such pretty smiles. I'll give you a dollar if you'll smile for the camera."

"No, man, we couldn't take any money from you. We'll smile for you anyway." So we all lined up and we smiled for him, and he came up with his Polaroid and he popped it for us, and he pulled it out and waited for it to develop, and it developed out to be just completely black.

"Hmmm," he said. "Too much light."

We looked at each other and giggled, as people did who were stoned, and in this mood we tripped on over to the Straight Theater.

When we got there, Kenneth Anger was on first. He threw an incredible scene. He was the guy who had done the flick, *Scorpio Rising*. What he was doing in the Straight Theater was essentially dark arts. And it was interesting what his name was. He had a series of altars around the Straight Theater, with a central altar in the middle.

Rockin' Jody had happened to walk into the Straight Theater while Kenneth Anger was setting up for his show. He came in, and there was a bunch of bad-looking altars around, with other stuff on them. So Rockin' Jody walked around the room, and he stopped in front of each altar and gave a long Bronx cheer. About the third time he did that, Kenneth Anger comes running out of the back of the hall, shouting,

"What are you doing? What are you doing?!?"

And Rockin' Jody just turned around and smiled and said,

"I'm stealing all your juice," and proceeded to walk around and go *phththththt* at all the altars, and walked out. He really had style.

81

When Kenneth Anger came out, it turned out that he wasn't going to talk. He came out and had a partner who was smaller. Kenneth Anger came on with threatening gestures to the guy, and the guy had an electric oud, a musical instrument with a belly like a mandolin and a long neck. It's usually played with a quill, but this was an electric oud, and he was peeling screamy, feedback screeches out of it, just bad dissonant sounds. And Kenneth Anger was coming on scary and threatening to the guy, who was writhing on the floor on his back, being submissive and coming on as if scared, and playing this wretched sound off of this electric oud. Kenneth Anger was wearing a full papier mache minotaur type bull head with horns. As this was going on, we chatted among ourselves and didn't pay good attention, and tried not to make it come on like a very big deal, although the sounds it put out were really screechy and hard to ignore.

Then he got finished, and Father Christos came up. Father Christos was a nice dude who worked for a yoga teacher named Subramunya, who we called Superdupe, a gringo who studied in Ceylon.

Superdupe used to take Father Christos out on this rock on Mount Tamalpais for these heavy ceremonies. Superdupe would be full-to-the-ground in silk and purple velvet robes. One of the reasons I liked Father Christos was that although he wore robes, they were plain brown monk's robes. He wore cowboy boots under his robes, and he had quite long hair. At one point, he had to tonsure his hair. Superdupe made him cut a big bald spot out of the top of really natural, long, waist-length hair. So he cut it and kept the fringe, still hanging to his waist.

Later on, Superdupe got down on hippies. There was so much magic, and he'd been wiped out so bad by so many acid takers, that he couldn't hack to be around them any more, and didn't want them. He said that anyone who wanted to do it with him had to wear a white shirt, short sleeves, and a black necktie, black pants, and black shoes. He put that on them, and all the guys who wanted to stay with him had to do that.

Father Christos stepped up and gave a really down-home and friendly and interesting rap about psychic energy and yoga and a few things like that, and in the course of it he showed beautiful colors of aura and put out a fair amount of psychic energy. We paid good attention to him. We looked at him like we liked him, and we made good closure for what he was saying, and we paid attention to what he was saying, and tried to help him out so he could remember his sentences, and helped him out the best we could.

He came back to us afterwards and said,

"Are you guys tripping? Are you guys high?"

And we copped that we all were high.

"Being up there with you guys was almost like flying."

We had socked so much juice to him that he had quite a good time.

We later went out with him and stopped at a vegetarian restaurant and had some juice and stuff, and tried to come to essential agreement. But our problem was that I didn't think I could join up with a yoga school or anything, even though this guy seemed like a good guy and I felt like he was a friend of mine. Even after I fell out seriously with Superdupe, I still considered Father Christos to be a friend of mine.

Father Christos came to see me on a Sunday morning in Stinson Beach. While he came to see me, the motorcycles came by on the ride I used to go on, from the Sausalito heliport out to Inverness. They came roaring past my house while Father Christos and a bunch of yogi friends were there. I was still pretty cruising on some left over of Saturday night's acid, and I was pretty banged. I looked over and Father Christos had my cat in his lap and was petting it. I could see, visibly, a ball of green light about the size of a watermelon surrounding the cat, and his hands were covered with it about an inch and a half deep. As he petted the cat, it laid layers of green energy on the cat. The cat was lying on its back, with his paw stuck up in the air, and its wrist at complete rest hanging down, mouth open, tongue hanging out of side of mouth, and I said,

"What are you doing with my cat?"

He looked at me with a startled look. Then he looked closer at me and he saw that I was pretty banged, and he realized that I was *seeing*.

"Manipuri," he said. "Manipuri energy comes from the solar chakra. Healing energy." And I saw, exactly as advertised in the books, literal green manipuri healing energy coming off of this nice guy yogi's hands onto my cat, while I had my acid glasses on.

Number Twenty-Six: The Double Helix

ohn had been my teaching assistant, and we had graded papers together. The course we were teaching together was General Semantics, so we spent hours and hours and hours of time talking about where people were at, going into subtleties of people from where their papers were at, and we had a rapport on a certain level that made it so when I tripped and he be'd my guide, he really gave me a pretty good guide. He knew sort of what I was going for.

It was the only trip where I had somebody who acted as a guide or a ground control. Most of the time that would happen, the guide would get contacted on so bad that he'd trip on out, too.

It happened to me because it was a special relationship. I was living on Broderick Street, with Margaret, in our fifth floor, illegal, technically nonexistent attic with no address. I decided I was going to trip, and this friend of mine named John showed up.

John was a Marvel comic reader, acid taker, motorcycle rider, and expensive shoe salesman at Bally Shoes. I knew all the guys who worked at Bally Shoes, because they were a little beatnik commune. They made a lot of money, and took a lot of expensive dope, and sold shoes to rich ladies during the daytime. They would hit up on Dexedrine or Benzedrine, and go out and just sell shoes to those rich ladies. A little magic going on in every direction in those days.

He sat there and chipped, and smoked dope, and I took a righteous hit.

He helped me out in a way, by just being a friend, and feeding back good stuff to me. I would just laugh and laugh. I was on one of those kind of trips where I understood stuff that tickled me so much that it made me roll around and laugh until the tears would roll down my face. And I would think of the sad corollary of all of that, and then I would cry for a little bit, not tore up, but a gentle, compassionate place. Then I would laugh some more. Then I was laughing and crying at the same time for a while.

It became all so obvious, and I had this inner vision.

The inner vision I had was against a deep background, like deep space. But instead of stars, there was a double helix, ascending and descending, to infinity, two spirals woven in together inside each other. And they were huge. Everywhere they intersected, there were lights. There were also some lights between the intersections; but there were lights on all the intersections, different colored lights; and the different colored lights meant things. And I realized that this was the DNA code that the trippers speak of, that this was the great DNA code itself.

I understood that one helix was the dance of the bodies and the genes, the gene pool, of life in its existence down through time. The other helix was the dance of the minds and the knowledge, and it was the other, equal, half. They were the two halves of the double helix. That was what we were doing, dancing down through it, with the bodies and the gene pool and reproduction on one hand, and the dance of the minds, the knowledge on the other.

I saw this, and understood it, and it was all understood automatically. It did not need any narration or subtitles.

I came drifting in from that vision very blown, and understanding just tons. I called,

"Margaret! Margaret!"

Margaret came in from the kitchen, and I said,

"Margaret. I have just discovered the simplest way to say where it is really at."

And I said this thing to her, which was the very essence of the experiences I had been having for the last couple, three hours out there. It was the very essence of it. I said it to her very cleanly, in one sentence.

Her face suffused with a glow. She looked as if she was stoned herself. She brightened up, and her eyes lit up, and she smiled a lovely smile, and she said,

"*Oh! That's beautiful!* . . . What did you say?"

I wish I could remember that sentence, myself.

Some Acid Aphorisms

Sometimes I remembered who I got it from. Number six I got from Vulcan. Number twenty-six, I got from a dude called Spade Johnny. Spade Johnny was a real, nice-looking young graceful coffee-and-cream black dude. I went to score some good acid. I was led to this house, up these stairs, to this room, knock on this door, talk to this cat. I bought one cap of it. I went home with it, and dropped it. The great DNA code and the works.

Really a grand vision. One of the purest visions. A benchmark.

Consequently, it always made me remember him in a good light. It wasn't like getting a handful or baggie full from somebody, and maybe one of them was good. This was like one guy going to one guy and getting one cap. And that was like he put his aura behind it, kind of guaranteed it or something.

It was like our friend Slim in British Honduras, who used to buy a fifteen-cent spliff from John Scorn, and turn around and sell it in front of John's house for twenty cents. He would smoke it with you, and if he smoked it with you, you got higher than if you smoked it by yourself. He was a good dude, and he was a tripper. He had several basic trips he liked to put people on, but he also could extemp pretty good. Everybody knew that they could walk right on past him and go to John and buy the same spliff for fifteen cents, but it was worth it to pay twenty to smoke it with him.

I remember some peyote I got from a crazy dude. Caps of peyote. I had thought of not even taking it, but I thought, *Well, peyote, man. Maybe the thing of the peyote will come through, and it won't be so colored by who I got it from.* We swallowed the caps, chickened out that way, too, so we just suddenly came on sick.

We were up on top of Mount Tam. I stepped outside the bus and looked back at it. We'd had the bus for quite some time by then, and there were a few rust streaks running down from the white paint. The bus just looked vile. It looked like Alice Cooper's old stained underwear or something. Dense fog, and all tripping, and the bus looked ugly. Everybody wanted to know if there was anything we could do. I said,

"Yes. There is one thing we can do, man. There is one thing we can do."

We fired up the bus, and drove down off of that hill, and we split.

By the time we got down into the sunshine, our karma had gotten enough better by the amount of attention we'd had to pay to don't drive the bus over the side of the cliff that we got smarter.

And we knew that it was just how we'd gotten that dope. And also it was that we'd swallowed it in caps instead of chewing it up righteously, so as to warn our stomachs.

I got a letter from the cat who said to me,

"Where there's dope, there's hope."

He's now dealing in Las Vegas. Cards, not dope.

That statement, and

"Grass gets you through times of no money better than money gets you through times of no grass."

We used to go farther than that. We used to say,

"Reality is a crutch for people who haven't got the courage for acid."

Sometimes we said that all the hippies left their bodies on Saturday night and went up in the air and came down in different people.

"I tripped yesterday."

"Oh yeah? You get on?"

"Yeah, I got on."

"Get off?"

"Naw, I didn't get off."

"Too bad, man."

There were hidden subtleties that people who took acid regularly shared as a lore among them, not as something out of a medical book or a textbook, but the real experiences from the street. Folks would say things like,

"Well, I usually trip once a week because I can *stand* it if I trip once a week. If I went two weeks, I'd grow enough ego in two weeks that it would just devastate me, blow me to pieces. But, if I go a week between trips, and really yoga in between, it's bearable, and I can stand it. I hate to skip a week."

These were acid aphorisms. And acid aphorisms were tough.

90

Electric Buddha

e were all reading books on weird mind disciplines and studying astral projection, and whatnot. Some of the magic was a little questionable, to say the least. One of my friends came up with a book on astral projection and how to get your spirit body loose. It was said to be by "Ophiel".

Ophiel, I recognized from my readings, was a name of a demon. Whoever was running this school had identified himself with a demon. I didn't think

91

that was too cool.

Way on down the line, I ran across that school again, and in a sort of a funny way. I ran across somebody who knew who was behind "Ophiel". "Ophiel" was an elderly and weird bachelor who sent out these books from a mail-order business run out of his room. He died, and his room was taken over by a prominent Haight Street methedrine freak, called the Electric Buddha, a strange dude who vowed to shoot methedrine until he attained enlightenment or gave up his soul.

The Electric Buddha moved into "Ophiel's" apartment. He reopened his mail order business, and people who then took the course on astral projection from "Ophiel" were in communication with a speed freak called the Electric Buddha. Probably no one was the wiser.

Hundred Button Tea

 ockin' Jody would always come up and lay something outrageous on me. He would walk up to me and say,

"I want you to try some of this dope. This dope was flown across the border by a one-eyed Tehuantepec Indian in a Ford trimotor."

He would lay some magic on it like that. Or he would come up to me and say,

"I don't care what you've been smoking. And I don't care how high it gets you. I want you to smoke some of *this*, which will get you higher."

That's what he greeted me with when I came to his pad in Sausalito one time, as I stepped into his house. He loaded up a pipe with Michoacan and set a chunk of white Lebanese pollen hashish on top of it. And he was right: it got me higher than I was.

He opened his bedroom door and asked me to step into his room. I started to step onto this nice green carpet that he had; and then I realized that it was not the green carpet at all: the entire floor was wall-to-wall, edge-to-edge peyote buttons, set out to dry in his bedroom—next to his closet, which was stacked full of kilos.

He was making hundred button tea.

A couple of the brothers from Haight Street were there. Ricky, and Joe, and C.R.; Aaron was there, and Rockin' Jody. They were going to do a peyote meeting with their hundred button tea. We were also smoking opiated hashish.

I was not being able to get the tea down very well, which they didn't think was very hip, and Rockin' Jody decided he was going to fix me up, whether I could get any tea down or not. He came over, opened up this bag, and poured out into the palm of his hand a whole bunch of different colored pills and caps and half-empty caps and broken-in-half tabs, all different colors and sizes and stuff. He said,

"Lookie here. These green ones were good. Take half of one of these. And here's a, oh, these were *great*, take one of these. And *these* were kind of good, how about one of these? Now, just take *half* of that one, I want to save the other half, ..." and just loaded me up on a bunch of stuff. I don't remember what.

I got to where I could drink tea a little better after that.

We began to get stoned, and suddenly Rockin' Jody and his friends began to look as if *they* knew what was going on, and *I* didn't. They went and got some stuff, and started unloading some things. They looked like they had tripped together before, and they knew what they were doing. It was pretty impressive, in that sense—because I was in a

94

place where I certainly didn't know what *I* was doing.

They came over and they had some stuff they gave me. They said,

"Take this and hold this. Keep it with you. This is yours now. Hold on to this."

It was a hundred-year-old Indian peyote bag, with beaded deer and stuff on it, an old deerskin satchel completely covered with beads all over the outside.

There was a white blanket, with yellow stripes on the end. There were some rattles, and chanting going on.

Jody began to talk to me in this sort of weird way, like an incantation. In a thing that was compounded of equal parts of straightening me, teasing me and blowing up my ego, all at once, he'd tell me,

"Aww, you're gonna do all right on this. A motorcycle rider like you, you're gonna be okay."

Jacking me up on all that stuff, which was actually symptomatic of the condition I had brought in to acid, the kind of stuff he was putting on me. I had ego involvement with it, and was taking some ego-hits off it as he came on to me. Rockin' Jody had been a lot of places.

At the same time, he was teasing me, and I was telling him,

"Don't do it!"

The thing he was doing was kind of tickling me in a way, and driving me stoned faster than I wanted to go. The kind of thing he was saying to me had the effect of making me stoneder and stoneder, and I was asking him to

"*Cool it.* Don't push me quite so hard," and like that.

And he wasn't stopping. He was continuing to push.

Whooaaaa! This is getting heavy.

Rockin' Jody holds up this beaded piece of Indian gear, as if it were a microphone he was talking into, and says, very seriously and solemnly,

"*I have authority for the North American Continent.*"

Somebody asked,

"You got the whistle?"

"Yeah," he said. "It's broken, but I think it'll still work."

He went and got an eagle-bone whistle, about three-quarters of an inch thick, nine or ten inches long, a great big eagle wingbone, broken in half in the middle.

He held the ends of it together, not even real straight, just holding them together, and blew this piercing, screeching, whistly whispy breathy note out of the whistle, and I was *instantly* kicked stoned. ***Bang!*** like I was kicked off a catapult. I went to a very stoned place, very high.

When I did, one of the brothers from the Haight looked at me and I looked at him and I saw that he was a pretty straight guy. Hundreds and hundreds of people who had met him at one time or another thought that he was a pretty straight guy, and whatever he asked was probably coming from all those people, too; and whatever you told him was probably going to be told to all those people, too. He looked at me with that kind of weight behind him, and he asked me what was going to happen.

I could just tell him what I'd been programmed with; I didn't have anything else to tell him. There had been a lot of laughing while they were jacking me up before they got serious about the ceremony, although I think the jacking me up was part of it. They had been saying,

"Boy, it's going to be outrageous. There's going to be kilos of grass around. Pickup truck loads full."

I was realizing that there was going to be *more* than pickup truck loads of it. There were going to be semi's full of it, airplane loads of it.

I couldn't give them quite the satisfaction they wanted—that grass was just going to do it by itself. I saw that grass had done a tremendous amount, but it could not carry a great social revolution by itself. I was very serious and very high and very strong, and a trifle sad not to be able to give it to them exactly like they wanted it; but I couldn't give them anything other than what I'd been programmed with: I couldn't make anything up.

From this place, I am high. I am *banged*. I am really stoned. And Joe's old lady comes over and looks at me. Each eye has a circle around it of neon violet, a ring like a small donut of vibes around her eyes—that's the reason why ladies paint funny colors on their eyelids, to try to make it look like that. She looked like Queen Nefertiti of the Nile. She looked like the Earth Mother. She looked like the sexy side of Mother Kali. She looked at me and invited me to be her friend, and to love her and be open with her.

It seemed the kind of relationship that I would have to ask Margaret about.

Some folks were saying,

"Nah, forget it."

And others were saying,

"No, go on with it."

She's saying,

"It's all right."

And her old man is saying,

"No, no, it looks like a paranoid bummer."

So I said,

"Let me try to ask Margaret."

This lady was so nice, and so good to me, that I have always loved her. When I met her again, years later, after having only seeing her briefly that one night, I felt like she was my sister. I felt like we were old friends. She had been good to me when I was seriously banged.

So I looked deep into her eyes, and started taking direct control of my hallucinating mechanism. I started painting her face over to be Margaret. As I did that, I tried to will her into being Margaret. I tried to bring about enough similarity between her and Margaret that if I asked her something, it would be Margaret who answered me.

I tried that, and I pulled with all the psychedelic power I had at my control. I pulled *hard* to do that, and I looked at it, and I realized that if I tried to ask it a question, it would be a monster. It wouldn't be Margaret, and it wouldn't be this one either. It would be wrong, and misbuilt, and I shouldn't try to ask it anything.

So I let go, and let it go, and it faded away.

I gathered myself together again. I pulled myself together, and I struck as hard as I could strike and tried to bring her to be Margaret so I could ask her a question.

Once again, when it came to a place where it was just *almost* looking like Margaret there was some little flaw in it that made me know that it would just be a travesty if I asked it anything. And I let it go again. I tried one more time. I pulled with all my psychic strength. The last time exhausted me, and I gave up and said,

"Naw, naw, I'm sorry. I can't."

They stripped me of the peyote bag they'd given me, and the rattle. Told me I wasn't worthy to have it.

I was still sitting on the floor where I had been when I was trying to reach for Margaret, and the air just *crackled*.

I thought I knew how to make it work.

I came on like I didn't have to change myself, I could change the system. And Joe went for me, knowing I was wrong and that I had to change myself and not just the system. So he went for me to prove that.

I went to try to prove my point. We began verbally, and transferred from verbal to telepathic.

When it went telepathic, it went in mind pictures for a while. The mind pictures didn't carry enough information at a time, and it started flashing of graphs. You'd see a screen and a graph, and an automatic understanding of the vectors on it and what it meant; and a screen, and a graph, growing and shrinking—and we were arguing in that medium.

Then we went from that level into anecdote, because that was the next heavy information carrier. When we moved into anecdote, we got into *plot*, and did burlesques of coyote and roadrunner plots, where I would be running away from him, and he was after me and on me and telling me he was right, and I would try to say,

"No, no!"

And I would, like, dive under the earth and take off a thousand miles under the earth, and I would pop back out from underneath the earth; and when I came back up, there would be a chain link fence around the hole where I came up, and he'd be sitting there tapping his foot, like Yosemite Sam, waiting for me.

I'd dive into some kind of math, and wade through miles of equations, brackets, numbers, symbols, and come out the other end, and he would be right there, already had it covered, already knew,

No. You're wrong.

And he had me cold.

I ran, jumped time and space barriers, did every kind of mind trip game I knew how to do, and there was nothing I could do. He had me cold. Because he was right. I couldn't get by with just changing the system. I had to change myself. And if I had been able at that time to change myself, we could have gone onto an interesting second half of the ceremony. But I was unable to change myself, and I was sent home in disgrace. A certain kind of initiation again.

I was technically disgraced. All my grace buttons ripped off my grace uniform, all my grace stripes torn off my grace sleeves, all my grace medals and ribbons ripped off and thrown away. Drummed out with a black-draped drum at a funeral pace.

Joe went over and stood in the corner, and chastised me, for being full of myself at a high place, and for blocking a ceremony that could have gone more smoothly. He never said a word. He did not say a single word. He just stood in the corner and folded his arms, and looked at me as I was sitting there on the floor.

As he looked at me, I gradually curled up into a little ball like the fetal position, curled down on my hands and knees, and put my hands on top of my head and tried to pull my head down betwen my knees, into a little ball, I was very stoned and his vibes were very heavy.

After he got done telling me that, I said,

"I'll try to do better. I've got more juice. I could get as high again."

And he said,

"Oh, yeah? We'll see."

He dipped a cup into the hundred button tea, and took a slug of it, and spit it out and said,

"Naw, it's just bitter water. Just bitter water."

And they sent me home. They let me off in front of my house, and sent me in to see Margaret.

I have never felt bad with Joe about it. I have seen him many times since then, and every time I have seen him since then, he was good to me. He was fair to me, he was not fake to me, he was true to me and he was friendly to me.

But I have to say, I was humble. They had done a number to me and got me humbler than I used to be, I tell you. I was so humble that I wouldn't say an original idea for three weeks. If I couldn't find scriptural confirmation, I wouldn't care to put it out. I was humble. I was backed *way* up.

Margaret was furious. She called Jody up and hollered at him,

"What have you done to him this time?? *What are you doing to him? Are you trying to drive my old man crazy? What are you doing?"*

She just wigged out at the condition I would come back in from these little seances.

The thing that was wild was, I told Margaret,

"Don't be mad at me, baby. I tried to ask you." And I told her about trying to ask her.

And she told me that in the middle of the night, she had woke up from a deep sleep with her head washed full of cool, orange fire. She said she had had three strong distinct waves and peaks of cool, orange fire in her mind. She knew it was me, and couldn't tell anything other than that it was me. Then it all went away, and she went back to sleep.

There was some kind of structure. It's ceremonial, yet

organic. That's one of the things I learned. All these guys who were going to come sell you a ceremony or an initiation or something are absolute fakers. Nobody sells you that kind of thing. *If you survive, you learn something.* Some of the initiations are ones where you survived, and learned something.

I came out of that trip blown, in a lot of ways. But I didn't quit. I didn't consider quitting on account of that. Margaret thought I was *crazy* for not considering quitting on account of that. But I thought I knew what I was doing. Not right away. Not for about three weeks. But after a certain point, I knew:

I am ultimately responsible for the level of consciousness and sanity of this here organism; and if I don't take care of myself, ain't nobody else going to take care of me. Because nobody else is going to really know where I'm at well enough to take care of me. I'm the only one who can build what I want built, so I am going to have to continue tripping until I build something I am satisfied with. And if I don't like this one, I will wait seven days and trip again.

Cut off Finger

ockin' Jody Morningstar was over at my house with his first old lady. I had a nice psychedelic vision on. Then, as I looked around, the vision that I had on began to disappear, as if it was being colored over with a crayon, and as if the crayon left not just a color, but a whole different picture. He got it all done that way except for one little corner at his lower right, which I could see out of the left hand corner of my eye, where he hadn't done it yet, and I was looking out that hole into my own reality. He followed the direction my eyes were looking in, and looked over at that little corner, and colored it in real fast with his reality. Then he smiled a fat sort of Chairman Mao, oleaginous smile, and said,

"Now, we're *very* stoned."

And I knew he was laying down a whole overlaid reality in front of me, which I just ritually didn't believe any of. But that was one of his kinds of magic.

We were tripping up in the Broderick Street illegal loft, and suddenly his old lady lay down on the bed beside me and started taking off her pants. She was a small, neat lady, had short hair and was a classical pianist. She was wearing corduroy pants and a brown sweater, looked rather like an English riding costume of some kind.

I was banged on so much acid that sex was unthinkable. I wouldn't be able to localize myself well enough to care to get into anything like that.

Jody was standing there at the foot of the bed with a frown on, saying,

"There's something very important. You have to make love to her. You have to make love to her now." And he pointed his hand at my crotch.

A large, bright white glow, about eighteen inches around, flared briefly over my crotch. And then he pointed at hers, and another white glow flooded over hers. And he told me that on account of these glows, that I had to make love to her.

I kept saying I didn't want to, this is kind of weird, and like that.

So he goes and asks Margaret, who said,

"I don't know. If you really think it's what he's got to do, I guess it's okay, but he doesn't look to me like he wants to."

As he stood at the foot of the bed and told me to do it, I felt myself psychically picked up and moved, hard, as if somebody had picked me up by the belt and jerked me up about six inches, then jerked me over sideways six or eight inches, moving my pelvis, which Jody was apparently doing

103

with his mind, from standing at the foot of the bed. And *that* was more interesting to me than the continuing question of whether to ball his old lady or not. It was showing me a lot of heavy psychic stuff.

What he was trying to do was to make me do a Sun Dance. That was what he was into. It was one of the old rituals, where the road chief makes love to the Earth Mother, either inside a buffalo skin robe, or in the open on the altar at a peyote meeting. This is one variation of the Sun Dance. The other variation is more the Lakota type, which is hanging by eagle claws pierced through your chest skin, until you tear them free. Rockin' Jody was all into the kind where there was some kind of sexual magic. on the altar. So he was trying to get me to do some kind of a Sun Dance with his old lady.

That was the same old lady who, later on in that same trip, took my hand in her lap, and I felt my finger cut off. I heard a sound, loud, like a scissors screeching through a blanket, and felt the pain, and looked over, and saw my finger cut off and gone, the index finger of my right hand, and a pool of blood on the floor. She jumped up and gathered the scissors and something else to her chest, and ran away from the bed fast. I watched the pool of blood change and fade and disappear, and my finger grow back on in place until it was there again and my hand was whole, and the blood was all gone. And she ran away to the other end of the room.

I would like to have known what was going on in more detail than that, but I was very stoned and they didn't offer me any more explanation. He put her through a lot of changes. I know some of the changes he put her through were some of the ones I went through, and I know they were heavy changes.

One time he said,

"Do you think I drove my wife crazy by treating her weird and making her take too much dope and stuff?"

And I said,
"Naw, Jody."
He gave me a contemptuous look and said,
"Joe from Haight Street does. I think he's right, too."
And he just left me there, with that insincere bullshit I had just said.

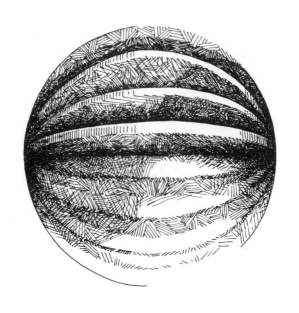

Flip a Coin

W e were tripping along at the loft, some people sitting along the edge of the window seat, some people sitting in chairs around the table, some guys peeling peanuts and dropping the shells on the floor, which irritated me a little bit. We were taking a bunch of acid. Paul was there, tripping along, kind of coming off a trip, past the peak and coming over a little. Lee's there, who's a southerner who talks a sweet southern thing. Button down shirt, short-sleeve wearing grass smoker and acid taker. Never grew long hair, always had short hair. Button down tab collar short sleeve— a crazy, psychedelic tripper.

Several other guys were there—Bob Fugue, one of the motorcycle-riding dope-doing shoe salesmen from Bally shoes was there, and another guy from Bally shoes who was a clean dude. His Marvel comic costume was white T-shirt, a powder blue cashmere sweater, short blond hair, and an angelic smile. He was always friendly. He was clean and shiny, and he knew it. He had a little bit of ego about knowing it, but he really was honest-to-God clean and shiny. You'd ask him about it, and he'd say.

"I'm just going to keep on trying to be good, man. I'm just going to keep on trying to be good."

He was a very clean dude. Looking at him once on acid, I watched him turn into a very beautiful saintly looking person, and hold it together for long minutes, much longer than you usually ever saw anybody hold their stuff together for you to see something like that. He was a beautiful kid.

Fugue was beautiful on the outside. He was beautiful like Marilyn Monroe or something. He was all voluptuous biceps, a handsome blond thing, strong, fast motorcycle rider, expensive hippy clothes.

Fugue at one point went over and lay down on the bed over in the corner, which had a light over it. He closed his eyes and began to hump a pillow gently. He began to say,

"Remember what it was like when they took you to the circus? Remember when they would take you to the merry-go-round?"

And he started this eyes-closed, loud-voiced reverie about some past trip about being at the circus, in some kid place, going to have everybody stop, shut up and have him, with eyes closed, not looking back, run that number. And everybody said,

"No, no, Bob. Come off of that."

Because it was obviously a figured out, completely

artificial mind-cop; and it shocked us that he tried to do such a thing. The clean dude said,

"Come on, man."

And then Bob looked up and said,

"You don't know what's happened to me. You don't know what's happened to my soul."

I said, "What's the matter with you, Bob? What's wrong?"

He had gone into this shoe store to sell shoes. He had become a hot salesman. His opinion about what would sell became respected. He began to be flown to Switzerland to pick out what was going to be next year's expensive seventy-five-dollar hippy dresses and shoes. He established a hippy shop in the basement called Bally Low, which became very chic and fashionable and made a *lot* of money; and he and all of his friends all bought new motorcycles and lots of hippy clothes and lots of expensive dope, and had a good time. They were like a mercantile collective. And he said,

"I have gone to these shows, and I have learned to fight for advantage. I have learned to counterpunch and be tough and bluff and intimidate, and use speed and acid for power—to buy dresses."

As he looked at me, his face sharpened into a tragic Fagin, the fence who was the teacher of young thieves on the street in Dickens. He rubbed his hands together in a cackle, and his chin and nose extended until they almost reached out and touched each other, and his soul was in a withered and strange shape, from having gotten caught up, stoned, in the money world, at a heavyweight money level. And we told him,

"Quit the job."

"Quit that job!"

"You cannot mix it."

"There's something to dropping out. There is a time, man, when you can not mix it."

We were so telepathic that we were all *connected*. We may

not have all been seeing exactly the same trip, but we were seeing the same analog, at least, which is a level of telepathy. Some of us were. Some of us were on their own trips.

Margaret called it the Yellow Submarine. She said the Beatles were there, we were tripping out through outer space with everybody. We were all part of the committee and very telepathic.

In the middle of this thing, we're sitting around and we're feeling tribal. People are looking Indianish, like various kinds of Indians. Margaret's looking like an Eskimo lady. She's sitting there swinging her legs back and forth.

Suddenly, Lee vibes loud and hard,

I want to trade you something for Margaret. I want Margaret, and I'll trade you something for her.

It was shocking in a meeting of that kind for him to throw out such a heavy acid obsession fixation lech. Earlier I had been sitting in the chair with Margaret in my lap. I'd feel her start swaying in a weird kind of way and I'd look over and Lee was sitting over on the floor at her feet, petting her calf.

I said, "Naw," and took it as a joke, and passed it off.

Then he talks about it out loud a little bit, too.

And I say, "No, no, no, no, no," with a little more resolve behind it, and a little bit stronger. And the idea bounces back and forth, and it doesn't get dismissed at the joke level. And it doesn't get dismissed at the *You're kind of pushy* level. And it doesn't get dismissed at the level of, *What about this here trip we're having?* And the people in the room start taking sides, saying whether that's a thing to request, or can he ask that? It's as if me and Margaret being together doesn't mean anything any more, and they're going to *decide.*

Various sorts of ideas in telepathic thought frames.

"Trade you some cows."

And I immediately step out of the tepee and slam the spear in the ground, quivering with the feathers hanging on

109

the shaft, and say,

"Our tribe don't do that."

Him following me around and pushing the idea on me. Some people getting leers. *Hoo hoo hoo, what's going to happen? A low consciousness.*

I asked Paul W. for some help. He was my friend. He wouldn't let me down.

This trip is going weird. I'm trying to get it together.

He said,

"Sure. I can help. Give me another tab so I can get some juice on." And he pops another tab in a very devil-may-care fashion.

I go off into the kitchen for something to eat, and when I turn around, Lee's right there. He comes on to me very heavy,

"How 'bout it?"

Very intimidating. Blowing my mind that anybody would come on so pushy and intimidating and try to move somebody around about something like that. Try to walk in and rip you off of your old lady by apparent, psychic, in-your-face force.

And then he says,

"How 'bout it, man? I'll flip you for her."

And as he says, "I'll flip you for her," a vision appears of an eighteen-inch disk, red on one side and blue on the other, which he takes in one hand and flips towards the ceiling. As he flips it toward the ceiling, the red and the blue of the sides become a yang and yin. It flips up, and as it comes down, he looks in my eyes very closely, and I look in his eyes very closely. He's looking in my eyes to see if I look to see which way it's going to come up. And I'm looking in his eyes so he can see, *I ain't going to look at which way it's going to come up. I ain't even going to look.*

And his face, as he pushes and strains against me, turns transparent, candle-waxy, and begins to flow and run in little blobs like a melting candle all over his face. Vision

110

partly compounded of real drops of sweat running down his face, but multiplied psychically until it was melting and running like the witch in the *Wizard of Oz*.

But I did not look, and he knew I didn't look.

That seemed to settle it.

We went back into the living room, and Paul W. is there, standing under the light. He's high, man, he is vibrant and strong. He was a very vibratory dude. Small, five six or so, very well-built, well-coordinated. Shoulder length red hair in a pageboy. Naturally athletic. Standing there, high, and gassed on it. At that point he has some kind of weird little, not-important-at-all, little ego quirk that makes it so he's afraid he can't just naturally say,

"Wow, man! I am *High!* I can do magic! I can see miles! I feel like a God!"—which was what was in his heart of hearts. He couldn't say it that way. He had to say,

"Here I am, I can do all these things, and it's not enough. It doesn't seem like anything to me. It isn't really fulfilling."

I had a vision of him where he was huge and golden-auraed, and about seven feet tall, bouncing like on a spring board, while he was saying all this stuff. He knew he was vibing at the same time, so it wasn't a totally backwards statement. It was sort of a wry irony on top of what should have been self-evident. He was so wild that he became what he said.

He said all that hogwash because he was afraid that if he said the open thing that was in his heart, he would be thought to be on an ego trip. And at that moment, he wasn't on an ego trip, until he elected to choose this little subterfuge to try to mask his joy by saying it through a mock complaining attitude.

I watched him do that having dropped on top of peaking, and start a slide/crash from that point that ended with him in a very sad condition. He was a really smart, well-coordinated psychedelic tripper. A starship tripper, who tripped at that speed, and missed on one mistake about not being true while you're that high, and tumbled.

They say the secret words of the Masons are, **I am**. And you be very careful what you say after you say that.

An Oriental Gentleman

There was this young dude we were tripping with in our fifth floor illegal apartment on Broderick Street, who was a great big dude, broad-shouldered, thick black hair, a big handsome young hippy—about eighteen or nineteen. He hung out with me. We were high on acid, and talking about our agreements about reality so as to have any idea of what kind of a base we could refer back to if we were going to create any kind of a system, which is to say, to try to be moral at all.

And suddenly this young, square-jawed man disappeared

in his chair, and completely replacing him, not like blotted on over him, or a picture floating like television keyed in, but as if there were a different chair there, in that place of the room, which had a four-foot square purple cushion with gold tassels on the corners, upon which was sitting a seventy-five or eighty year old golden-colored Oriental sage in beautiful robes, purple silk with red frogs closing it and a small purple pillbox bishop's type hat on, who looked and said,

"Perhaps if you didn't consider the greatest good of mankind as the greatest good, you would have a chance of solving the problem."

It was very stoned, and very cryptic at the time; we almost got it, but it didn't quite...make...good...sense... the way it does now. It was really about the oneness of life. Not just man, primates, slow loris, but the trees, and the grass, and the monkeys and the mastodons and everybody. We were really all one thing, and any violence done to any other was violence done to life; and as long as we considered the greatest good of mankind as the greatest good, we could destroy our planet.

It's taken me years to understand that as well as I understand that now. But, boy! He just jumped right smack-dab in the middle of our argument, and it wasn't that kid who said that. That kid didn't know that.

Then, when it was said, he vanished. The kid was back in place. I don't know where the kid was during the transaction.

We said,

"Did you see that?"

And people said they saw that. It was, if you will, a group shared hallucination, if that's the sort of language you want to use. But we saw that.

114

The Stinson Beach Trips

e rented one of the biggest, nicest houses in Stinson Beach. Big, tall, two-story pillars by the front door, a big huge old thing, and a grove of pine trees that was host to a herd of Monarch butterflies all year round, and really a lot of them sometimes. The canyon that came down the mountain was full of nasturtiums, so there would be this piney woods with this great white house sitting up in it, with an orange river of nasturtiums flowing down the mountain, and the air full of Monarch butterflies, and lots of hippies on acid floating around the house and through the woods. It was really a place for a while. There were a lot of weird trips that went down at that place. That was where I scared Margaret's mother back up her tree, trying to get her high.

My daughter Dana was a good friend for me. At Stinson Beach one time, I was on acid and the other guy was not, and the other guy sat down beside me and gave me this earnest little lecture about how every team has to have a quarterback, and that it was him, and he was going to call the plays, and like that...

While he was doing that, Dana was running along the beach, quite young and innocent, and the sun was just behind her and the waves had just washed that section of beach with water, and the sun was just coming off the water about as strong as it was coming out of the sky, so she was running along through this intense white light; and all my consciousness, and all my aura and all of my trip was over there with her, and what was sitting here was just one ear, and the rest of me was just astral projected. And she had *all* my juice, and he wasn't ripping me off of anything, because I didn't have any of it. She had it all in this intense white light.

She was my only true tripping partner in a couple of really heavy trips. There was one of them where I told her to go outside and play, and she said,

"It don't feel any better out there. I'd really rather be with you."

She hung out with me while I was coming on when I had been dosed by what I think was something approaching 3500 mikes, a very strong amount of acid, that had effects on me that were just incredible. That same day, I had been filling up a gallon jug with a hose, and it had the male screw-on part at the end, which was just about the same size as the inside diameter of the gallon jug, and I had the hose stuck inside the jug. It just filled right up, and when it got to the top, it just popped the side of the jug out, instantly, before I could pull it back out.

116

Then, later on that afternoon, I was sitting there on this acid, and thinking clearly that the back of my head was about to pop off, just like the side had come out of that bottle. Just thunderous, rushing, roar, an amazing head of steam. And then,...

Hmmm.

Dana, Rockin' Jody, and some other people were there. I was *high*. I was really sailing. Jody came up with some grass, and we were cleaning it in a wooden bowl. It was really good grass, and you could see the grass fall the way sticky grass falls. It looks like huge mountain ranges crumbling and having avalanches, in small proportion, when sticky grass crumbles and breaks. So I was deep into that, and somebody came up and asked for something, and something happened, and I made a fast, smart-ass remark from that stoned place.

It kind of brought me down some, and I realized that I had kind of blown it, and was trying to get it back together. And while I was trying to get it back together, I suddenly came under attack from this young guy. He started putting it on me like Dana had wanted my attention, and I didn't give it to her, so I was a real bad cat, and he put it on me for a long time, considering that I was peaking on a real lot of acid. Like,

"Ho, Ho, ho, little girl, take care of the little girl."

He put it on me in this funny way, making a hassle between me and Dana, which didn't really belong there. I wanted to be friends, she wanted to be friends; we loved each other. We were a little island, her and me together, in a way.

So I went through these changes with this young guy putting it on me, and finally I just said,

"Me and Dana is okay."

I picked her up and went into the living room. Jody was there, and he saw that I was in this emotional and highly-charged situation.

He came at me and started waving these eagle feathers in

these magical patterns at me, pushing me, fanning me, waving me along down the path, sailing down towards a heavy ego death, behind that same acid that I had been afraid I was going to blow the back of my head off with. I'd tell him,

"Please don't. Please don't push me."

It was like mild-mannered David Banner, but I wasn't afraid I would turn into the Hulk; I was afraid the Hulk was going to get *me*. I was just tripping fast, and near my time, and I was trying to arrange myself so it would be cool. Here I was, holding Dana in my arms, and he's there waving these eagle feathers at me.

I was standing there, and I suddenly hit the edge, and it was like hitting a stone wall going a hundred miles an hour.

I was standing there, talking, arguing with him, saying, "Please don't."

And suddenly, I felt my entire spirit come up out of the inside of me in one *Sob!*. It came out of my toes and my fingernails and the ends of my hair and through my whole body—every cell gave up its ghost at once. It all came up out of me through my heart and out my mouth in one big sob that just emptied me of life.

I crumpled, and I fell.

As I fell towards the floor, Dana *loved* me.

My vision had gone out of color and was losing integration and going into greeny posterized-looking black and white.

And when she loved me, I saw red come in. It scared me at first, because I thought it was blood. And then it kept coming, and it suffused the picture. And as it suffused the picture, it brought a kaleidoscope...and renewed life and color.

It was a clear vision of the sacred heart.

When I saw that light and that color and that beauty come back into it, I knew that Dana's love and the love of Christ were the same.

They talk about little children, and trusting little children. Dana's pure out-of-her-heart love was just like the love of Christ and I was saved by the love of Christ right then.

Midge thought I was too old for Margaret, because I was her college teacher. I was trying to make friends with her. I felt like, in that naive way that someone does in the early days of acid, that if I could get stoned enough, I could contact her off so hard that she'd get stoned, and then she'd understand, and everything would be cool. This is a very naive attitude, as I later found out.

I saw Midge outside. She was a good-looking lady, young, as pretty looking as Margaret. I started to walk over to talk to her. And she walked away from me.

I saw that she was going around a little piece of woods by a road, and I could cut across a neck of the woods and meet her by the road. So I cut across and met her there, and it just wasn't any good; she just didn't want to talk.

I went back in the house, and I was getting stoneder and stoneder. I was sitting there in the living room, which was a bright room with a fireplace in the side, all painted white, a bunch of San Francisco Victorian gingerbread molding around the plastered ceiling and walls. High windows with a lot of light coming in.

Midge came in and sat in one corner in a high, straight-backed chair, a real good-looking, strong looking lady. I was sitting diagonally across from her, in another chair. And I thought, *As stoned as I am, I ought to be able to throw a vibe over there that would stone her so hard that she would like it.* So I tried. I reached out, and tried to stone her. And I saw that it was going all wrong. As I tried to stone her, she thought I was trying to cop her mind. She thought I was trying to take her over or something. I didn't want to take her over, I just wanted to get her high. But she was afraid I was trying to take her over, and she be'd very brave, and very strong in the face of this, which to her was an assault.

I picked up with as much juice, and made it as high and bright and light as I could, and the room almost began to melt and flow. And the first time it even just shivered a little bit like it might melt, she seized up real proud and straight like a queen, and held on and *froze that room* so that no psychedelic phenomena could take place in that room. That room was going to stay that shape—that tall, that wide, that long. There was going to be no variation in the architecture or the geometry what-so-*ever*. She froze that room tight while I sat there and revved it up, and it sat there and looked like an ordinary room, preternaturally illumined, until I finally saw that I was making it worse the harder I would try, and I gave it up and quit. But she didn't talk to me or feel good about me for five or six years.

That same night there was some hundred and twenty dollars worth of acid taken in the house by one folk or another—they decided to burn a ouija board. They thought they'd been truckin' with the wrong kind of spirits, and they shoved this Ouija board in the fireplace, and it went Crash, Bang, Noise, trip, wild, weird vibes of destruction and fight, a real scene. I turned around and said,

"What in the *world* was all of *that*?!"

"Oh, we just burned the Ouija board."

There was a night when an old friend of mine named Lloyd came to visit, who thought that all the hippies were pretty fluffy and fancy in their paisleys and flowers, and he'd been psychedelic for years behind a white tee-shirt and blue

120

jeans. He stood in front of us and became a white comet with a blue tail just *streaking* through the Universe, just showing us what a little of his plain old blue-jean and tee-shirt style was like.

He did a little piece that reminded me of Sakini, from *Teahouse of the August Moon*, where he said he just wanted his little piece, and he didn't want any of anyone else's. He did it with a little dance, where he delineated a little island, and showed how that little island was really very small, actually just the ground under his feet. He pushed everything else away as if it were waves, and he was rolling the waves away, until he was standing in this one little place that was his own little place, and that's when he became a white comet and *shwheeeeewwwwwwww!* showed us his stuff.

I was telepathic as I could be, and having a good time, lying back on the floor and watching a few folks.

Dale, of Larry, Terry and Dale, was standing in front of a room full of tripping people. He looked something reminiscent of Country Joe and the Fish, and was lip-synching singing Hot Damn Vietnam. He made the most intense teenage bad-mouth gestures possible, to show his approval of Country Joe's anti-war song.

I got into a girl's mind who was very uptight about being Jewish. She didn't know it, didn't believe it, didn't want to hear it, but there was like a closet in her mind, full of old musty praise and blame and fear, where she was uptight about being Jewish. I got pretty telepathic with her. It didn't hang her up from getting pretty stoned herself and being telepathic, but it just didn't free her up. It was very deep-seated. She got very stoned in other ways. I looked into her eyes and she broke into a blue third eye between her eyes, and then it began to multiply like sections of stained glass window adding on to the pattern until it turned into a triangle that covered her whole forehead, a great big old stained glass window that covered the whole top half of her head, a sky-blue, lit-from-behind stained glass window

121

looking out at you.

I saw Lloyd lay a nice healing on Paul W., after Paul had lost his nerve on that trip on Broderick Street when I asked him for help. It was the first time I'd looked at him closely since that trip. When I turned psychedelic and looked at him, it looked like his head was banging back and forth from shoulder to shoulder, the way a punching bag does if you slam it really hard, slamming back and forth against the stop on both sides. It looked like his head was a half-circle, from shoulder to shoulder. It was like an outline of the edge of his face, then another eighth-of-an-inch, and another edge of the outline of his face, then another eighth-of-an-inch, and another one, just eighth-inch fractions, like a fan spread out. Schizophrenically *fractured*. And scared. And uptight at me because I wasn't very compassionate about his being scared.

Lloyd showed me a pretty good lick. He came up and said,

"Jesus said when he was asked who he was, if he was the son of God, he said 'I am one of you.' If that's true, what he said in that fashion, then any one of us is the son of God, and I'm a son of God here as I stand in front of you. And you and I can make contact if you don't have contact with anybody else in the world. We can establish a friendship and look at each other and smile and talk,..."

And he got Paul out to smiling and talking, and Lloyd said,

"Now there's this guy sitting over here beside you on the couch, who you aren't paying any attention to. Let's include him in on the conversation."

And he got this other guy in on the conversation. Then he got another guy, and got Paul so he was out from where he was, less self-absorbed and less scared, and Lloyd said,

"Now continue to widen your circle of acquaintances until it includes all sentient beings."

Now that's funny. I saw him do a piece of magic like that, and he has been mad at me and down on me for years. He's a little mad about prison. I tried to let him know I understood after I'd been in prison, but he didn't want to listen to me.

He said,

"This engine runs on LSD and peyote, and it also runs on booze and heroin and sniffing gasoline and cocaine and Romilar,..." He just did anything. And he had some incredibly bad trips he told me about some times, like ending up underneath a car in an underground parking garage, quivering in fear and hiding, creeping out from underneath the car to a phone booth, calling someone to pick him up, telling them how to check into the garage, come to certain row number, open the back door, and let him crawl in, turn around and drive him away from there—because he was so scared and paranoid.

On the other hand, when him and another teenager were busted for dope and hauled away to some California mental hospital, they hung by their knees from the overhead pipes, and flapped their hospital robes like bat wings and pretended to be vampires, and weirded out all the people in the hospital. He was an old time revolutionary dude, in a lot of ways.

One night, a kind of drunk guy, a little obnoxious, wandered in in the night. He went up and crashed in Lloyd's bed. Paul W. and young David and I and one or two others were banged on acid in the living room. Lloyd was not stoned, and he wasn't stoned about this drunk in his bed, either. At the time, I didn't understand what was happening very well; but it looked to me as if somehow we had been remiss in our duties in taking care of this person. Lloyd came busting into the room, saying how we gotta get this cat out of here. I asked Lloyd to handle it on account of we're *stoned*, and tripping our tail off.

In the course of figuring out what to do about this guy, it looked as if we had done something wrong by not taking care of this dude properly. But in retrospect I realized that the dude had been in Lloyd's bed, and what Lloyd had done was to shivvy all us acid takers who were stoned into doing his work for him to unload this guy and ship him off so he could have his bed free. But I didn't see that at the time.

We went through these changes, and the guy got obnoxious, so obnoxious that we finally said,

"Look, just split. We're not going to have you here fighting with us while we're stoned. Just go ahead and split."

The dude began to split, and as he got to the door, he opened the door, stepped out with one foot, looked back at us, sneered and said,

"Some kind of Buddhists or sump'n, huh?" And turned around and slammed the door and walked off down the road.

We were left standing in the doorway with that, and we walked back into the living room and sat down in front of the fireplace and looked into the fireplace, and the ashes in the fireplace turned into maggots: the fireplace seemed to be full of a mass of crawling maggots in all those light, grey, white ashes. We had violated among us, those of us in that house, not just Lloyd, not just me, not just any of us, but all of us together, the house had violated the sanctuary, and had violated hospitality. And our hearth had turned to maggots.

We got back out of that. We didn't stay there forever. But that's where we got to.

At the Stinson Beach house, Rockin' Jody was sitting on the couch and said,

"You know, to be a rock and roll band these days, you

124

hardly have to know how to play music or anything. All you have to do really is just walk out on stage and be *outrageous.*"

And when he said "outrageous," sitting there on the couch, he turned into a human-sized two-headed chicken with gold beaks, and *lederhosen* with embroidered suspenders. He was outrageous.

That was the sort of thing he would do. That was one of the things that was fantastic about his telepathic ability. He didn't do that stuff on purpose; but it just took the spirit of what he said and made a picture of it.

One time he said he was going to do something about a grass deal. He said,

"Now my associates and I..."

As he said that, the background of the house behind him turned into a walnut paneled boardroom, with pictures of old guys in Hoover collars and cravats, oil paintings around the wall, the board of directors he was apparently referring to as he said, "My associates and I."

On another occasion, possibly in the same place, he said,

"I'm having such a hard time with dope because I'm just pledged to Ricky, and he just sucks me dry."

As he said, "sucks me dry," he shriveled down into a little bitty inch-wide thing that was just a head, like a life-sized real head, with his body shriveled away until it was only an inch wide.

Those were some of the telepathic effects he was capable of producing.

Jody had a cat that was the prettiest Siamese male cat that I had ever seen, or that anybody I ever saw who ever saw it had ever seen. It had lines like a tiger. It had a chin on it like a tiger, which stuck out. It had a powerful chest. It was well fleshed-out, but you could still see its muscles ripple out through it, in his shoulders and his haunches: a beautiful Siamese cat. Jody called it his Ng cat.

He and his Ng cat went and had an acid trip up in Mendocino county with John Sure, and Jody said he was

125

poisoned. He said the acid had strychnine in it. He said it was anything at all but good acid, and that something had been done to him.

To all his friends who knew him, from listening to him it was obvious that he had gone on a trip while stoned, and had gotten himself sick, crazy and out there from being on a heavy trip while stoned. And the thing that really cinched it for all of us who knew him well was that at some point during the trip, the Ng cat left him, and never came back.

Some nice kids would come hang out with us. I think Margaret picked them up and brought them out to the Stinson Beach house, which was Shangri-La for some folks. The whole house was pretty stoned on acid.

Vicky and Debbie—it seemed like everybody was named Vicky or Debbie in those days—were playing a game, standing on either side of me, where I would let my head sort of float, and they could cast out and see if they could catch my head and drag it toward them. They got a hold on it, and it would start going toward Debbie, and then Vicky would turn it up more and it would start going toward Vicky. Then Debbie would turn it up a little harder and it would start going toward Debbie. They got it going back and forth between Vicky and Debbie, and it turned into a tug of war and quit being fun. But we realized that we could touch and pull on one another with our minds.

Then we were sitting in some kind of small group, tight around the wood box in a corner of the room, four or five of us scattered around the wood box, and we shared a vision of flying rocket ships against the night sky, and we knew the rocket ships were our minds. They were screeching across the background, leaving trails behind them, going fast and cutting tight corners, doing aerobatics, and I heard Larry say,

"I wonder how fast you have to run one of these to blow it up," in his teenage hotrod way.

Terry and Dale said,

"Yeah, yeah," and it began to be a feeling of revving and pushing to some sort of limit.

I realized that we weren't supposed to try to blow them up. It was not a good thing to do. I backed out, and said,

"I ain't playing this game. I ain't interested in trying to blow it up."

Larry and Dale went back to their families. Terry became a rock and roll drummer, and may be a hippy yet.

Ned was a fellow who had run one of the rock halls in San Francisco. In the course of running it, he had become a wheeler-dealer. He had a similar breakdown to Bob Fugue; but his took the form of a permanent bum trip, which he went on for four and a half months. He walked up and down Haight Street, dirty, filthy, gray and grimy, looking like a shot out speed freak even though he wasn't taking anything at all anymore.

He had two speeds: complete apathy, and the most gross arrogance of ego. He couldn't stand himself when he was full of ego, and he dragged around in apathy because he couldn't stand his ego.

We picked Ned up on the street, found out what kind of shape he was in, and took him out to Stinson Beach. One of the first things we wanted to do was to see where he was at if he had any energy on, so we dropped mescaline together. The mescaline got him stronger, but it didn't make any difference. It just pushed him farther into the ego side. He showed us a little of the ego side until he couldn't stand it, and he retreated back into apathy.

I told him, and everyone else agreed with me, that we thought he could come back from that; but that what he had to do was to be really selfless, and really take care of somebody else. We tried to give him instructions on how to do it, but he passed us up right away. He found the spirit of the yoga, and he put it together for himself.

What he ended up doing was, he was the first one up in the morning, helping straighten up the house, square away before breakfast; he was usually the last one to go to bed at night, helping put the kitchen together for the next morning. He slept outside on a thin mat with a sleeping bag and rose with the sun. He made sure everyone in the house was fed before he ate, including the animals, the pets.

He worked out like that until he attained a kind of self-sufficiency. Although he was still a little down, he was probably the most competent person in the house by that time. No one else was taking as much care.

Then he said he needed to be more on his own. Even though he did all the work he could do in our house, even being in our house was more support than he wanted. So we arranged for him to get to use a boat that belonged to a friend of ours. He moved onto the boat, and we gave him fifty pounds of brown rice. He fished for fish over the side of the boat, and stayed in the boat and meditated and ate brown rice and fish, until he got interested enough to walk into Sausalito some times and see what was happening in town.

The last I heard, he had a van with a stereo in it, a girl friend—had drifted back out into the real world. Put himself back together. It took months and months to do it; he put himself back piece by piece, and came out somebody on the other end.

Park Ranger at Tam

he energy was very manifest, and as Jimmy Durante says, *everybody* wants to get into the act.

I was tripping on Tam, and I can barely remember the trip. But I remember leaving and coming out the little gate at the parking lot, and meeting a California State Park Ranger in green park ranger clothes, a serious looking crew cut about three quarters of an inch long, a little heavy. He began to talk.

"You boys been up the hill, eh? Had a good time? Yep. Well, I'll tell what folks don't know, though. These hippies come up here with their dogs. You got any dogs?"

"No, we ain't got no dogs."

"Well, a lot of these hippies bring their dogs up there, and one time those dogs came up, and you know what happened? Right back up over that hill over there a pack of hippies' dogs, German shepherds and stuff, got down a mother deer and the fawn, and tore 'em to pieces, back there in the clearing."

He proceeded to describe various aspects of this event to me, as I was there tripping hard, harder than I'd expected. I had thought I was done tripping, but I found myself tripping hard, trying to keep a sense of perspective, trying to stay high, trying not to lose the vision I had brought down from the mountain, trying not to be uptight with the park ranger, trying to understand, trying to share his feeling about how badly he must feel about having those two deer torn up, wishing that hippies wouldn't bring dogs to Mount Tam, having a hard time about it. I went away feeling bad about that.

I was coming down off of Mount Tam about a year and a half later, off of another trip on the mountain, and I came back down off the mountain and ran into that same park ranger. And I recognized him. But he didn't recognize me. And he began to tell me this story about how these hippies bring their dogs up this hill into the park.

"Right back over that hill there, some hippies' dogs, German shepherds and stuff, got a fawn and a doe, and tore 'em to pieces."

While he was telling it to me, I realized that it was a practiced story, and that he had said it a lot of times. Maybe that had happened once, and maybe it didn't even happen. I realized that this was one man's answer to the hippy problem, to catch every one of them he could coming down off the mountain, and bum their trip.

130

He was the troll at the bridge.
Trip trap, trip trap. Let me over your bridge.
Not until you pay.
And he made us pay coming out of his park. Park Ranger.
Park troll.
Trip trap. Trip trap.

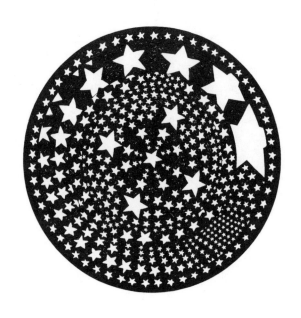

Two Tabs at the Straight Theater

In those days, they were having a little trouble on Haight Street: the City wasn't quite cooperating as much as they could, so they could not get a license to be a dance hall; but there were licenses for dance instruction studios. So they said they were a dance *studio*, and they were going to *instruct*.

The way they did that was, Santana came up on stage just like it was going to be a rock 'n' roll dance, and a whole bunch of people came out on the floor like it was going to be a rock 'n' roll dance.

Then Rockin' Jody Morningstar got up on stage and said,

"*This* is a dance studio, and *I* am the dance instructor. I am going to teach you guys to dance this evening," and he gave a few instructions about dancing and stuff, and said,

"And we'll start off with *this* little dance..."

As I had come in the Straight Theater slightly before that, Rockin' Jody had met me with a baggie of caps of acid, which he was supposed to go around and hit people in the audience with, to make it be **stoned** *at the dance. We were very direct. I came there, and I was a friend of his, so he hit me with a couple of them. So I did these two hits of this acid. It was a righteous five hundred mikes.*

So Rockin' Jody got up and said,

"All right. This is the first dance we're going to learn."

He got everybody out on the dance floor holding hands, in a big circle. Then he had me go stand in the middle of the circle, while I was coming on to these two caps of acid. Then he had them start dancing and daisy-chaining in one direction, and he had me start spinning in the other direction; and he had Santana start blowing a set. We danced a set like that, while I spun in the middle and the crowd went the other direction holding hands, and wound up this psychic generator.

When we got to the end of the set, Rockin' Jody came walking out on the floor with a smile on his face to see was I *stoned.*

I looked at him, and through him to the wall. When I hit the wall, I tilted my head back and looked at the fancy-painted ceiling of the Straight Theater. I looked at that; and then I looked through it, and I saw the fog above the ceiling, and I went on out through that into the stars and the universe—it was like my mind was a searchlight that reached out into space for thousands of miles, out through the roof of the Straight Theater.

"Whoooooew! I am *very seriously banged,* here," I thought.

Zeke, my country friend from Alabama, said,

"Hey, I have some friends in a band who's playing. Let's go hear them for a while. "

So we left Santana and went into a little country music type bar. We went in, and there was a band on stage. I don't know all their names, but one of them was Fast Eddie. They were playing, *My Pretty Fraulein*.

I was sitting back by the piano bar, in an overhanging alcove, kind of out of sight and in the dark, and people couldn't tell how seriously stoned I was—because by that time, I was in the eyeballs-clear-across-black-holes stage.

While I'm looking at the Styx River Ferry playing *My Pretty Fraulein*, it looks to me like the ceiling opens up and God looks in. And that the Styx River Ferry's higher selves become aware that God is watching the set, and they do an especially good job for Him. This Presence just seemed to look down in through the ceiling, and we'd look back up at It.

The Styx River Ferry was a psychedelic band. Their name had meaning. I felt like I was having an ego death, and the Styx River Ferry was rowing me across the creek. That was their bag.

After the set was over, I started to split. It was hard to walk, I was so stoned. I came past where S. and O. were sitting at the bar. I knew them from creative writing school, when we used to hang out and drink coffee and read our short stories. We all started taking dope the same time. They kind of went this other path than I went, and I never saw them very much. They hung on into being writers.

At this point I probably would have considered myself a creative writer, a writing student or something. As I was unching out down the aisleway—the place was pretty crowded—I got behind these two cats, and I got to hearing their conversation. I was so stoned, I felt like I was almost invisible. I felt like I was Ebenezer Scrooge being privileged to witness a vision to teach him something, and that nobody really knew that I was there. I mean they knew I was there, they'd said hi, and went on with their conversation, about

"All them other writers is no good," or

"Wait until they see my stuff," or

"Hemingway could really knock them all out of the ring,"—just all this real, college-y writers' idea of what a writer is. It was such a complete bogus, spurious trip—and it was me. I wasn't separate from them. It wasn't me sitting there judging them. It was me and them. I was them, they were me. As they talked, they unraveled my ego between them, and talked about my ego until I was just *fried*. It touched something deep inside me that made me know that I was not a writer, and I would never be a writer, and I should just give up all that old bullshit. I have never thought of myself as a writer since, and don't consider myself to be one now.

That blew me away, being—as some heavy trips are— keyed to things in yourself.

After the set we got invited over to the band's house for coffee and probably a number.

On the way over to the band's house, I saw that I was still pretty seriously blown. I had a perfectly clear shot of a hippy stepping off a curb in front of a bus, which apparently hit him. Then, as the bus continues on down the street, it comes off the hippy who is still standing there, as if one of them were not material. I don't know whether the hippy wasn't material or the bus wasn't material; but they were in the same space at the same time; and the bus from one plane hit the hippy in the other plane, and it didn't make no difference. They were not mixable.

We got to the Styx River Ferry's House, and there was a stoned party going on. I was in that acid integration place where the house felt like the inside of my skull. It felt like every conversation in the house was my own thoughts working themselves out. I didn't have to say a thing, just stand there and listen to all these different people talk to each other, and those were my thoughts. They were also

135

their own independent conversations. But it all matched together perfectly. They said things like,

"Oh, there's a lot of juice in the photography shop tonight. We ought to be able to take some pictures. There's a lot of juice in the shop tonight."

Which seemed to me to refer to the amount of psychedelic energy that was ambient among that bunch of stoned people.

Then they brought me a stack of pictures to look at. It was about an inch and a half thick. I went through the stack. As I went through the stack, they were nice pictures. I could flip through them rapidly, one by one, flip, flip, flip, flip.

Suddenly I came to this one picture that was much like the rest of them—they were all photo-snapshot sort of pictures. But this one had a somewhat different texture than the other ones. It had a picture of a guy in a cowboy-looking fringe coat, standing beside a great big rugged tree.

The picture caught my attention instantly. I looked at it, trying to understand what it was that was doing it to me.

The talking near by me fell to a hush, as people looked to see which picture I was looking at, and what I was going to say.

As I looked at that picture, the bark on the tree made a little latticework of diamond-shaped sort of holes. There came, suddenly, a living, flesh-and-blood, twinkling face with eyes looking at me out of each of the little diamonds in the bark on the tree. The tree was like a Tree of Life, and all the faces were the folks who were holding it up. The guy leaning against it was part of the tree, too; the whole tree and him became like faces looking out.

"Who's that?" I asked.

"He's this good dude who lives in L.A."

I gave up the stack of pictures, and they took them away. I heard someone in the next room—Fast Eddie, I think.

"What was the picture he stopped on? Which one did he like?"

136

They showed him the picture. When they did, Fast Eddie did a physical back flip from standing where he was, and fetched up crashing into a pile of chairs in the corner of the room.

At that, attention seemed to pass from me. The party continued on, and it was time for me to go. But I felt like something had been done, like there had been a connection made; and that wherever I went, I was somehow connected to this good dude from L.A., whoever he may be. I felt telepathic with him when I saw his picture.

I started home, and there was something heavy going on.

As I left the house, Fast Eddie says,

"Go for broke. Put your foot in it as hard as you can. But don't forget where the brakes are."

And we drove off down the hill with that advice. We crossed the Golden Gate Bridge, started up over Mount Tamalpais out towards Stinson Beach, a winding, curvy road along Highway One. It turned into dense fog. You could barely see through the windshield of the car—you could just make out one dot of white line on the highway ahead of you.

I began to have these feelings that maybe something awful had gone down out at our house. A paranoid feeling I'm sure others have felt, like there's something awful going on somewhere else that they have no control over.

I turned on the radio station, and it seemed like there was a warning of something ominous happening. Zeke was mad about something, and was driving along with an angry attitude on. And I was being blown by that, coupled with this feeling of impending doom. It felt like the guy on the radio was speaking my mind, listening to the radio station. I got very stoned on that.

I decided that this was too crazy. I couldn't hack being this crazy. I was going to fix my attitude and pull myself into a good trip, whatever the outside circumstances, I wasn't going to roll along bumming like this.

I pulled myself together as hard as I could, and convinced

myself that everybody was really all right, and tried to bring myself into a good, strong, adult, intelligent, loving kind of a place.

As I did we drove instantly out of the fog into clear, moonlit night.

Once we got home, although I had already made a good enough decision about it to get myself high, I still had to be sure.

I walked through the house, and I went to each person's bedroom. I put my hand on them, and felt them be warm and felt them breathe before I went away to the next one.

I made sure everybody in the house was warm and alive and okay. When I could feel all of them and they were all okay, then I could relax and let my thing down.

I was ready. I was very stoned. I had been tripping so hard for so long. My friends took care of me, and brought me into a re-entry; and I ran into Rockin' Jody again, who was over at my house, waiting for me to come back from wherever he had sent me.

Chloroformed by the Hell's Angels

few semi-trailers were pulled up for a stage at a boogie in Golden Gate Park. I was listening to the rock and roll sitting behind the stage and a whole group of Hell's Angels came walking through the crowd.

The hippies were pretty used to the Hell's Angels and weren't scared of them so it wasn't too scary a scene. But, as they walked by me, a great big, bearded, head-banded Hell's Angel and his black leather vest with the sleeves tore off and his Hell's Angels colors on the back suddenly takes a dirty motorcycle grease rag and claps it over my face and puts his other hand on the back of my head and says,

"How 'bout some chloroform. Did you ever try chloroform?"

I sat and tried to hold my breath as long as I could, but I eventually had to breathe and take a few whiffs through that rag. Then he took it off of my face, looked into my eyes, smiled and said,

"Like it?"

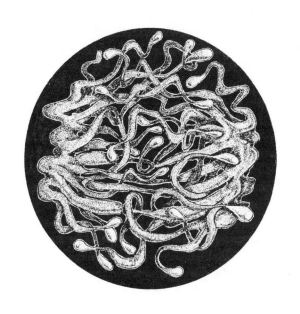

Psychedelic Bob

s near as I can remember, Psychedelic Bob showed up at Stinson
Beach while we were stoned, and
said that he had heard about me
and had come hunting me, to see where I was
at. He was in his late thirties, an executive in
San Francisco, who wore a suit and tie by
day, some straight job, and he had this guy
who he lived with. They were a couple who had been
together fairly stably for a while. Bob's friend had the worst
bad mouth. He could put out moans of despair and wails of

anger, sneers of contempt—boy, could he put out bad mouth. He had vibes like a whiny old witch.

They both wore black racing leathers, of the very severe kind, no decoration—not like Hells Angels' jackets, but like a high Russian neck, one zipper down the front, zipper on the cuffs, no decoration—smooth, black leathers.

These guys showed up, and at first I thought they were kind of quaint, because they were so obviously square and dresssed up. Then, as they talked, Psychedelic Bob—well, we didn't call him that at first. This guy started talking about dope and mind, and he was good. He was tough and he was smart; he had read a lot, and he had tripped a lot; and he had had a lot of heavy trips. But he was cynical, in the place that to him the power all seemed to be in the Left Hand Path, and that was what he really followed.

He told dope tales while we were stoned. He'd rap on me while I was on acid. It would be a place where he would get my acid attention, and I would hear what he was saying, and there would be an exchange like that; but then I'd notice that his tales and stories all had a certain kind of point, and a certain sort of ending.

An example of that was the time we talked about Nikola Tesla and broadcast power. He came on strong and broadcast some power. And then he said,

"Of course the thing about broadcast power is, once you get the power out there, and everybody has the power and wants to use it, you have to figure out how to *bill them for it.* You have to have some kind of a structure, or you won't be able to bill them for it."

He'd come on a little angry and a little scary, and start trying to throw down a network of control on a bunch of stoned people.

I watched him, and I learned from him. And I'd wrassle with him when it seemed appropriate, and I would just listen to him if I didn't feel threatened, and I went through a lot of changes.

When he went away after that first day, he had talked a lot of stuff. He went away, and the next day we were saying,

"You know that dude who was here yesterday?"

"What dude?"

"Bob."

"Bob who?"

"Aw, man, *Psychedelic Bob.*"

So that was Psychedelic Bob.

I never knew his phone number or anything. He would just show up, usually while I was tripping, like Rockin' Jody. He would show up with his guy, who would never say much, but just sat around and moaned a bad-tempered obbligato to whatever it was that Psychedelic Bob was saying.

Bob had read a lot of Evans-Wentz, and dropped a lot and like that, but one night he came over and he just wasn't nice. We didn't mind it too much. I had a gang of young hippies stoned around me, and we were pretty strong, and didn't care much about how he was. We just let him be part of the trip, and he was tripping along with us. Friends is who you trip with, regardless of where they're at. He was one of my friends. He was a competing magician who was after my tail all the time, and didn't give a hoot for me no way, except insofar as he could use me for a marker to measure his ego against if he could waste me. That's all he cared about me—but we were friends at *that* level.

We knew where it was at. It was like a couple of people cooperating in a venture, building something together over a period of years, and both going armed all the time, not being sure enough of the other to go unarmed; but there was a *relationship*, nonetheless.

Then a couple of kids that had been Freshman English students of mine showed up, popped into this here party at this pad out here in Stinson Beach. They had just taken their first acid trip, and came out to see me with their first acid

143

trip on, transcending along in all kinds of eighteen-year-old squeals and giggles. And I thought,

Boy, Bob had better be nice. With this sweet young thing in here on her first trip, I don't want to throw any weird stuff down on her.

And when I checked out how Bob was, he wasn't nice. And he wasn't going to be nice. Him and his guy were already beginning to rev up the moan. They understood about agreement. He brought someone along to agree with, help him get his manifestation started.

I decided,

Well, if it's a question of agreement, we've got some agreement here, too.

What we'll do is we'll just hippy him right on out. We'll just flower child right on through, here.

So while they were sitting there in their black leathers, going to be black magic and mean, we went and got all the Beatles records in the house, and since several of us had gotten together from different houses, we had several copies of each of them, so we could put them together side one, side two, side one, side two, side one, side two, a whole stack of them, turned them on wide open, all kinds of bright, loud Beatles music crashing through the house, turned on all the lights in the house, closets, bathrooms, pantry, everything, turned on all the lights and got it bright and lit, and went up and gathered all the beads and bangles that had ever been laid on me in years and years and took them down and hung them around everybody's neck until everybody was all hung up in beads and bangles and all, and then started passing out a little dope.

These two guys over on the couch split a cap, each doing half of it. Psychedelic Bob turns to his friend and says,

"Hey. They're dropping again. We'd better get out of here."

And they just jumped up, got themselves together, and split—just behind the power of a lot of bright light, loud music, people boogieing. We threw a little flower power down on that one.

Another night, he came back, and everybody had gone to bed. It was just me and this guy and Lee, who had been going to rip me off of Margaret on Broderick Street. The fire had gone out in the room. It was cold. Earlier in the evening, there had been a few more people around, but they had mostly split. One cat had been sitting there. I turned to him from the fireplace, and looking at him was like looking into the fireplace. It was like looking into hell. I saw some pride that came into peaked eyebrows, like peaked roofs, and a lot of definition in the beardline, so it made little batwingy points along his cheeks and chin, and it looked like he was exhaling a little flame out of his mouth. He looked pretty rough.

I looked at him, and I didn't say anything, but he read it off of me right away. He said,

"Oh, don't look shocked. There's a little bad place in all of us, isn't there?"

And I thought,

"Say whaat?!"

And I watched this cat's progress, because he was an intelligent dude. I watched him run down to a very sad place, shlepping around downtown in white jeans with a brown stripe up the back, soaked through from the inside, just really burnt out, burnt out. He was riding his ego on a long sled ride downhill, and he got worse the longer he stuck with it.

Psychedelic Bob would try to do stuff like spells. He started putting it on me,

"And then there is this force called Abraxas, which is *more powerful than* **God!**"

He's saying more powerful than God, and starting to vibe and spread himself and come on pretty strong, trying to evoke this here Abraxas. And I thought,

Contradiction in terms.

This does not compute.

145

God is totality.
Totality is all.
Nothing is outside the All.
There are not two things.
There is only one thing.
Bullshit on your old Abraxas!

Then Lee hears all this power talk coming off of Psychedelic Bob. Suddenly, he rears up and says,

"Power? Power?" and changed into an angry deity. He became like four feet across the shoulders, and a great brass chest plate cuirasse with all kinds of deep carvings on it; and a helmet like a Buddha's helmet in that it had little knobs all over it, like rivets that stuck out of it. His aura was made out of all kinds of weird colors that didn't go together good—greens and purples, a set of colors that you learn to recognize as the anger colors—oil-slicky colors around the temples when they get that way.

He was putting out full-dress, full-armor Mars war-god aura, full angry deity. And then, in this voice that was like one of those computer-synthesizer-augmented voices in the spook movies, he said,

"*Power?* **Power?** *I hear talk of* **power,** *but there's nobody here but* **people! Just people!!**"

His head was in a weird place. I had cause to wonder where he was at a couple of times that night.

On one occasion, I looked at him, and instead of him sitting there was an eight-foot-tall green worm, about eighteen inches thick, all reared up on its hind legs, obviously intelligent, and looking like it was from outer space.

So it got pretty weird in the corners during the course of the evening. Finally, I got to where I needed some help from my friends.

Pamela's bedroom was upstairs over the living room. When Bob would sneer and be contemptuous and growl and be pissed, and his guy would moan and wail and banshee behind him, and the room would turn dark, and it would rain blood and cinders out of the ceiling, I would take a deep breath and I would reach real hard, up into Pamela's bedroom. I would feel her vibe, and reach for how she was then. And little pink hearts and flowers would come floating down from her room. And I would pull hard on the hearts and flowers.

And we went that trip all night. In the morning, we went out on the beach, and looked up. The sun was just cracking over the hills out into the cove where Stinson Beach is. It was very Zen-like and very beautiful.

Bob turned around and looked at me. Then he came out with a pair of finger cymbals out of his pocket. He looked at me intently and suddenly *clanked the finger cymbals.*

I felt—*Flash*—a wave of fear. He just threw a wave of fear at me just like a Doc Strange character: *Whap!* He became threatening, and tried to sacrifice a piece of my aura to the dawn, by scaring me loose from it.

I saw where he was coming from. I saw that to engage was to give him my energy. I said,

"Good morning," and walked back into the house and left him on the beach.

When we came back into the house, I told him,

"You can go home."

They left then.

As I learned more and more, I learned that he was a fear magician.

One time, after I had left Stinson Beach, and we were living in the place on Day Street where we took off in the Metro truck from, in San Francisco, in the Mission, he came over with an obvious challenge.

"I want you to come with me. I have a record I want you to hear. We want to prepare you for it."

It was an obvious challenge. It was something spooky.

Margaret said,

"Don't go. Don't bother with them."

147

But I felt like it would be fun. I wasn't uptight about it at all; whatever it was would be fun. I had been tripping my *tail* off for a while, doing all these changes, and I had metamorphosed to a place where I understood his magic pretty good, and felt pretty immune to it.

So we went over to his pad.

His vibes were funny, and he was weird. He got out this little bud, and he introduced it with that it had made people afraid. He talked about how this grass had scared people. That was his trip, making people afraid.

So he asked me to listen to this record.

I said, "Sure."

I lay down on the couch, and put these earphones on, and put this record on. It was a talking record, about somebody going through a heavy trip—being captured by somebody like the Nazis, going through a lot of heavy things happening to them, a pretty spooky record. It goes through to where you're going to escape, and they escape and they're getting away, and while they're getting away clean, suddenly, *Bang!*—they're caught again. It was a real mind-bender.

I figured it out and went to sleep in the middle of it. He came in to see if I had paranoided out by being stuck full of a lot of heavy grass and being thrown, highly suggestible, into a weird situation. He found out that I had dozed off, that it hadn't been scary enough to keep me from going to sleep.

It was kind of funny, because his magic evaporated a lot. But he knew some things.

Later on, I met a kid who was his chela or student. I saw that Bob was running a little school on his path. He was a seventeen or eighteen-year-old. He was funny. He came on patronizingly to me, that I was self-taught:

"Pretty good for self-taught."

He came on like he'd been taught by an expert.

That kid knew magic, too. He knew a funny way to sing, where you sing offbeat from what you're playing, in an off-

148

rhythm pattern that gets you stoned in a rhythm like the song by Donovan about the Hurdy Gurdy Man. It's a far out kind of syncopation.

This kid could play guitar and just scat words off it that way, and *stone you*. And cop your head. He could hypnotize you that way. And he had been taught. There were people who did magic on purpose in those days. That kid is probably tougher than any psychologist at Vanderbilt or Harvard.

That was the way it was. People were all trying to learn magic, because it was obvious that it was real. I felt that there were certain clues in it—such as that you don't seek for magic. Seeking magic is almost like going armed, in a way. But you seek righteousness, and when magic comes along, you don't shrink from it, and you don't be afraid to *wield it* if that's what's happening, but you don't search for it.

You can't put magic above love.

Many Fireplaces

Rockin' Jody liked to do more magic than he did with me, and he would come to me, and tell me weird stories sometimes, that I was supposed to just believe, or take them or leave them, or what. One time he came in all wild and crazy looking, with eyes black all the way across on Methedrine and acid, and told me about how he had been stopped by a cop, and had suddenly quit talking the conversation where the cop was busting him and begun a new conversation, and the cop began with him on the new conversation, and forgot about the one about him being busted.

He would tell me these stories, and I would say,

"*Jody!* Not only should you not be doing anything like that to anybody's mind and free will, but don't even *tell* me about it, man! You make me an *accomplice* to this piece of *black magic*, man!"

And he would just gleefully recount these weird reports to me about copping policemen's minds right in their faces.

Another time, he came walking in the house in Stinson Beach, and I was there with a few young guys I was tripping with.

Jody came walking in the door, and there was a starburst of bright light floating about ten feet over his head. I looked at him, and said,

"What in the world are you doing?"

He said,

"*I...am...illumined.*"

And I said,

"Your ass. You ain't even *nice*. What *is* this?"

After I had badgered him for a while, he finally copped that it was Methedrine that he had shot up on. He was on a typical speed/power trip.

He came in and sat down. We sat in a circle in the living room. It was a bright, sunny day, and Rockin' Jody looked at me, and his face became round and fat, and he looked like Chairman Mao again.

Then that faded away, but I took it as a signal to *watch out, we were tripping*, when he began looking like other things.

He said,

"Nice fireplace you got there."

When he said that, he shot a three-foot tongue of yellowish-white flame out the top of his head.

And I said,

"Yes. We *do* have a good fireplace."

And *I* shot a three-foot tongue of white flame out of *my* head.

151

And he said,

"Only room for one fireplace in a room like this."

And his vibes began to spread away from him like ink blotting through paper. His aura began to grow and increase.

I said,

"We have more than one fireplace here. We have a lot of fireplaces here." And I waved my hand.

And all these young hippies sitting around shot eighteen-inch flames out of the top of *their* heads.

His vibes continued to flow up from his side of the room, and go out towards the middle. My vibes came up from around me, and I saw my vibes coming around the sides of the room and towards the ceiling, heading towards the center of the room, and I saw his vibes coming up over the walls and the ceiling, heading towards the center. And his vibes and my vibes met, in the center of the room, and they came together and fingers of them slipped into each other. They began to flow into each other, and they resisted each other for a while, but they broke through and flowed through, and it was one manifestation created by him and me and everything there, sharing it and holding it in our minds.

I knew that we were in that kind of place it talks about in the *Bible,* where when they talked in tongues, it didn't mean babble. It means the universally understood tongue. All this babble is a bunch of glossolalia.

We accepted Jody into the thing. We maintained our integrity and created a unified environment that we all could exist in and maintain our free will in. We had to step lively and we had to give all the right answers. If I had opposed Jody myself, and not drawn attention to the potential of the flame in all of the young hippies who were also there, it would have been a dichotomy, and when our vibes hit the ceiling, they would have frozen into two halves, and then we would have gone into sudden death overtime.

152

It was like psychic akido. The kind of thing where somebody twitches, and the other guy sees what that is going to be when it flowers into a movement, and he begins the movement to counter that before it has begun to flower.

It was like that. Not much time to argue. Not much verbalization.

I was seeing myself in interior and exterior vision. I was localized in my body, looking out and seeing the room through those eyes, and seeing the flames over Jody's head and over the other kids' heads; and I was also somewhere in the middle of the room, seeing me and the flame over my head. I was in that room, omnipresent. I think that's where we all were, where we all ended up being.

We weren't in a hassle when Jody came in. He brought a hassle, and we had to solve the hassle. But after we had solved the hassle, it was okay.

I knew instinctively that those tongues of flame were kundalini flames, and when we said "fire place" we were talking about a set of open chakras or energy centers. For him, there was only room for one set of those in a place. And that was how I began to learn to teach the opposite of that. That was one of the places where I learned that there had to be room for *everyone* to open up.

153

Ravi Shankar Concert

he City was so stoned that *everybody* knew there was magic afoot. Even the square folks knew there was magic afoot. Lots of square people were getting contacted on. Many policemen were being contacted on, by the people they were arresting. There were freaky scenes going on in police stations and interrogation rooms, where guys were getting seriously contacted on and weirded out by people who were very stoned.

There were mass trips where thousands and thousands of people got stoned together. Everybody who was there got stoned, those who dropped and those who didn't. At some of these mass stones, amazing things happened.

One of these I remember very clearly. We decided to go to a Ravi Shankar concert. We were living at the big white house in Stinson Beach. Five or six of us piled into a white Volvo I had at the time, and went to the Ravi Shankar concert.

As we left the house in Stinson Beach, we thought,

Let's drop now, so we'll be nice and high when we go into the concert.

So we each dropped on the way in. As I was coming over the top of Mount Tam, I began to hallucinate so hard that at each curve I had to look at all the alternate universes and pick out which was the one the car could drive on, and drive on that one. It was okay; I brought us out all right. It wasn't really dangerous, but you had to look now and then to see where you were going—as various illusions dance past the windshield, and your reactions are so wild.

When we got to the concert, I had a strong stone on. As I came in, I felt myself disturb the room, which was already pretty quiet. Ravi Shankar was up in front, tuning. So we sat in the back, and I sent out a little prayer that went like,

I don't want to be any trouble.
I know I came here stoned on acid to a spiritual thing,
And I don't want to ruffle it or anything.
I don't want to be any hassle.
All the energy I came in with, I want to give to you,
To do your thing with,
And I'll lay back here and be cool, and dig it.

It was like a little prayer between me and Ravi Shankar and his drummer onstage, to try to make peace with the vibes, and not come in with a great big old acid jangly drive-over-the-top-of-Mount-Tam vibe on.

He began to tune his instrument. As he tuned his

155

instrument, he played one note sometimes again and again, and then he would tune it again, trying to put it back exactly on the note he wanted it on. And sometimes you would listen, and these notes would go into your mind, and you would feel like,

That note is just for me. If he hits that note that way another time, I'll think it is for me.

He did it.

If he hits that note another time, just that way, I'm going to know it's for me.

And he'd do it.

And you'd think,

This is too much synchronicity. If he does it again, it's going to be outrageous!

And he would do it.

He didn't know me. He didn't know I was in the back of the room. I was one of the vibes, in the ocean of vibes in front of him. I felt very cleanly that he was tuning my vibe. And then I felt him, just as cleanly, let go of me, and the tuning didn't feel quite so personal. He was tuning someone else.

He began to play. He went through a couple of ragas, and we got kind of stoned. When we got to the sexual raga, we were very stoned. The entire inside of the Masonic Auditorium was very high right then, with thousands and thousands of people inside there, and many of them were stoned. And a lot of them were squares who were not stoned. Except that by that time it was getting pretty psychedelic in the whole room.

A couple of times, through the ragas, there had been a feeling as if someone was fighting Ravi Shankar. There would be this clank, thud, clank, like two great heavy objects hitting together underwater, and the whole field of vision of the entire inside of the room would just jolt a little bit, and vibrate a little bit, and settle back into still again.

He began the sexual raga, and as he began it, he spread a

156

beautiful, clear, sexual vision. I began to hallucinate with the music he played. As he played, it was like he had spread a veil, and there were beautiful bodies, smooth, clean, healthy, rosy, not-dirty, Holy, beautiful, and *sexy*. Dynamic, beautiful turn on—he brought it right up from the earth.

And then there would be the sensation of that great jolt, as a bunch of people would be unable to handle the vision that was being spread. It would crash, and it would look as if there were tomatoes and rotten vegetables being thrown against the walls of the Masonic Auditorium, replacing that clear sexual vision with splashes and garbage running down the walls.

And it would turn dirty, and cartoon, and ugly.

Ravi Shankar would let go of that phrase, and would go back and start again. He would start with something simple, and start building. And when he got it building and got it going, he would spread the vision out again. He would spread it out, pure and clean and sexy. And then there would be this big fight over whether we, several thousand people in that room, could experience that vision. Would we be allowed to, or would our collective subconscious not allow us to?

Then there was an intermission.

We went out into the lobby, and the bright lights, and the longhaired people and the shorthaired people, and square people and hippy people, looking in each other's eyes, thinking,

What in the world is going on in there?

Nobody would talk. The whole lobby was quiet. People stood around, lit cigarettes, looked at each other. But they didn't talk. Because if they did, they would have to talk about what was going on inside there. And when the intermission was over, we all just went back in, and settled down, and went on through the concert.

He integrated us very nicely, Ravi Shankar did. Towards the end of the concert, he was moving along. There had been a few more jolts and crashes, like astral earthquakes—I expected to see the pillars part and the ceilings fall from the jolts, but they were just astral.

Then he got jamming so hard and so fast that you had to follow him. You couldn't hassle with him. You couldn't judge him. You couln't criticize him. You could barely stay with him. He was sailing. He had us all moving, everybody in the place moving so hard and so fast, and sailing so free— and suddenly, before anyone could do anything about it, he reached out in front of the drummer and slammed off the last note on the drum:

Whap!

And it was over. And we were all home free. We were out of the fight, on our own clean karma. He brought us out of the trip clean, and turned us loose.

Everybody understood what he had done, and the incredible skill that he had shown to bring us together to trip together like that. We all shot to our feet, screaming, hands in the air, cheering, and we came back out of that place like a happy army, smiling and laughing, and got-off and stoned and banged out of our mind, saying,

"Man, if you were in at the thump, you were *in*. You had to be in at the thump, man, but *everybody* got in at the thump, man. He knew everybody was ready and he did the thump, man. And if you were in at the thump, man, you were *in*!"

So there were people who went home from that concert with a lot on their soul that they had to think about. Some of those people were tripping too—even the ones who hadn't taken anything.

Doctor D.

octor D. and I were real good friends in a way. I liked him because he was *smart*. I went through a lot of my major changes while knowing him, and as I got to know him better, I realized that he basically tolerated me, that I was kind of an interesting extra in his cast of characters.

Doctor D. was tough, partly because he was so well educated and so sure of himself. He knew a lot of weird magical jive, but he had learned it from very classical sources, and had it very well organized, and was very together about it. Somebody who knows the philosophical underpinnings of the principles he's working on when he's doing it to you is much tougher to deal with than somebody who's just expeditiously grabbing what looks like a good thing to do it to you with.

I would go and see him, and I had some stoned trips once in a while with him or his old lady. On one occasion I remember Doctor D. being faintly contemptuous of how stoned I was. I had found some excellent grass, and had brought it over for the purpose of getting Doctor D. high. I wanted him to share the experience that I was having such a good time with. I had enough grass for four joints and we smoked those four joints in a row.

Doctor D. was apparently not stoned at all, although I was helpless. Doctor D. sat and looked at me with a small cynical smile, as I rolled the four roach ends of the four joints into one last joint giggling helplessly and weakly, saying,

"A four motor bomber, hee, hee, hee, a four motor bomber."

I drank over at his house a lot, and would get a little drunk sometimes. He did a funny kind of a thing that shows what kind of guy he was. I had bought a brand new motorcycle, a 450 Honda, the seventh one in San Francisco, really hot on the road, everybody wanted to know what it was, it was a screamer. I dropped by Doctor D.'s house while I was riding it around town in the new, and he conned me out of riding it and into going out with him and his old lady for dinner in a fancy restaurant instead. When I got done with the fancy restaurant, I took off and rode from San Francisco to Occidental, leaving San Francisco at midnight, to go ahead and do my interrupted trip, which he had taken me off of doing by taking me to this restaurant where the tab was seventy bucks or so for three of us.

I look back on that, and I think he just turned me around

to see if he had enough juice to turn me around when I had that much enthusiasm on. He just did that as an experiment. He was a *practical psychologist*. Not nice, but practical. His line, *Not nice*. He told me about some other guys who are not necessarily nice. He said,

"Don't you think if there's anything in psychology that works, there are some people who are going to misuse it, just because they know it?"

He was such a double-leveled cat that he was telling me that and doing it to me at the same time, waiting to see if the half of my brain he was trespassing on was in communication with the half he was talking to or not.

There is other stuff that he just taught me in the academic fashion. He wrote a little paper for Hayakawa which said that a baby deer knows to freeze and hold still when something threatens in the environment; it becomes part of the environment and hangs tight until the mother comes and finds it. But to a human baby, the outside environment is meaningless: the mother is the environment; and if the mother is cool, the baby is cool, because the baby and the mother are a co-system together.

Another one of the little papers he wrote said that if you ever see anybody who is really messing up and you wonder why they are, look at how *well* they are doing it. Which was just him.

People do stuff on purpose.

I was living at Stinson Beach when this trip went down. I had been over at his house in the afternoon, hanging out with his old lady. I had had good stones with her; she was fun to get stoned with. We got very wrecked one time, reading the *Encyclopedia Britannica* on reefer, which says,

"Although there are many called hemp, there is but one true hemp, and its name is *Cannabis sativa*."

It goes on and on like that, until we became morally certain that it had been written by some hemp-head, who had laid in much heavy earth-mother-Goddess respect in it—

161

the description of the seeding process was so sensuous that it sounded like the *Song of Solomon.*

When we tried to read that to him, it was hard to make him understand it. Because he understood it perfectly.

He understood what he chose to. He had a ponderous intellect. Stoned, in the sense of heavy, granite chiseled intellect. Half-buried, covered with moss. Felt burnt with the world. Knew he was one of the smarter ones, and how come he wasn't really out there? He'd done a lot of stuff. He'd been California Democratic Party Chairman in the early-'thirties; he was a millionaire; he knew all kinds of newspaper leftists like Paul Jacobs—I met Paul Jacobs at his house at a party. The guys who worked for *Ramparts* when *Ramparts* first got took over from the Catholics hung out at his house.

I got into this trip one afternoon when I got stoned with his old lady on some good reefer, and she saw my aura, or said,

"I see your aura very plainly. This is far out. I can really see an aura on you right now."

I felt pretty stoned, and I believed her.

She said,

"Could you come back? D. would *love* to see it."

I said, "Aw, good. I would really like to show him that. I'll go home and get Margaret."

I went and got Margaret and Dana, and came back. We put Dana to bed downstairs, and I dropped two caps of this pink acid, five hundred mikes, figuring that I would charge up an aura he could *see.*

As that came on, early in the trip I felt good and very banged. I talked about how good the revolution was going, and like that. I felt very revolutionary. I felt clean and strong and peaceful. In fact, one of the visions that came through was of me standing knee deep in San Francisco State College, barefooted and wearing white pants torn off at the calf, and a white peasant shirt—Mexican revolutionary

162

peasant style of garb—a very romantic image, but I felt part of the hippy revolution, and felt good about it. I was exuberant in it.

I showed Doctor D. a few things. I did kind of a dance of Shiva for a moment there, where I turned myself into an energy ball, and started controlling the energy. I thought I was creating a level of vision he could see. At some levels later on, I *know* this was going on, but that's what I was attempting to do, just directly throwing visions at him on the power of all this acid, figuring if he was telepathic he'd get some of them.

Then I sat down in the chair across the room from his desk. There was a little fireplace in the corner, and a picture window at one end looking out over Twin Peaks in San Francisco. Classy art—Paul Klee signed prints on the wall, Mondrian, very simple, tasteful, expensive. His desk had a black leather and polished wood sling chair, with desk lamps and a door for the desk top, and hanging shelves above that, covered with books and papers.

We sat and talked, and I began to have sort of a *deja vu* because I was coming into this conversation that I began to recognize. I started to realize that this was a conversation I had been through with him several times in the past, not really knowing that I had been through it before, or perhaps just dimly noticing it, and not bringing it up enough to think anything about it.

As it went along, it became less and less general and more and more specific, until it ran through a couple of verbatim sentences I knew had been down several times before, and had never noticed.

The sentences were a little question-and-answer thing between him and me about Hayakawa. He would ask me what I thought about Hayakawa, and I would say,

"I don't think Hayakawa is very smart."

And he would very clearly telepath at me,

"Maybe smarter than you, young man."

163

He thought I was very forward, to come on like that. After all, he was working for Hayakawa as a hired brain, and didn't like to hear that.

For some reason, he had chosen this particular set of questions and answers as his trial run, tuned as it was to my ego.

While I was noticing that, I saw that he had his hand under the edge of his desk lamp, and that the desk lamp was loose on its shade; I saw that by just moving his fingers up and down a quarter of an inch, he could make it so the light from the desk lamp shone in my eyes or just above my head.

I realized he was conditioning me with the light in the eyes, and that if I was going the wrong way, I got more light in the eyes, and when I got to going the right way, I got the light out of the way so I could see.

I realized that the time had come to get stoned with this man, to come to terms with him. He was a sufficiently skilled and self-aware psychologist that he was just running me through a lot of changes.

When I recognized that, the relationship with him really began to change. At first, I just sort of reared back.

He answered with this heavy power trip. He was drinking, and was kind of immune to my stuff, while I was very vulnerable to his. He started putting his hand over on the desk and miming like he was turning a switch back and forth.

As he would turn the switch back and forth, my consciousness would strobe, like jerky gritty hand-held battlefield movie camera, from-black-to-white-to-red strobe flashes, with blown-out sound like heavy artillery going off, blanketing my sensorium with a lot of real heavy static, while miming he was flicking a switch back and forth, and looking at me, and smiling.

That's a real paranoid construct, in a way. But there was enough stuff going on in the material plane to tie it together in a way that was very weird. At that point, I quit thinking of him as revolutionary, and started thinking of him as Establishment. There he was, conditioning away. And he did some other tricks.

Margaret and I both saw him change as he represented various factions by the accretion of civilization in his attitudes—he would look like people who espoused those ideas when he would speak them to us. He would look like LBJ sometimes, a great big old long hound dog face with great big old white sideburns; and sometimes he would look like Mao, and he would be round and oily, and dangerous and slippery. Sometimes he was a Nazi, and he would look cold and scary and psychopathic.

Various political extremes, such as Nazis, became not merely political parties, but planes of mind, syndromes for sure, almost diseases. Almost an illness, instead of a political party. The paranoia and the turned-off lack of compassion, and the fear—the Nazis were afraid. They were afraid a little curly hair was going to affect their entire scene. They were afraid that a couple of brown eyes were going to blow civilization. They were really afraid. That was one of the insights that Doctor D. sort of drove me into, because he said,

"There's something I see in you. If I end you, will it end?"

I said, "No-o-o way." And in my mind, I telepathically made a picture for him to see, of what it would be. It was like the world was a completely round ball, like an ocean with waves and ripples. And when you got close enough to see it, the waves and ripples were people, genes.

I dived like a springboard from where I was in Doctor D.'s apartment, and went straight into the world, right through the center, and popped through the other side. And I was totally different in every way, ... except ... that that still lived. I shed every characteristic and came up totally different, and still the same. It was through everything, and couldn't be ended.

It was like the genes. They lived. It was the DNA molecule, from a different perspective.

One of the characteristics of Life is optimism and good vibes. Otherwise, you'd just be a selfish, drugged robot.

For a man who had been a Leftist and a Democrat, he was appallingly monarchical in his subconscious. He did little object lessons in front of me. He asked me if I was some kind of a Celt, and got me to talk about the background of my name. And then he just pinned me like a butterfly, showing me all the ego I had in it, and all the specialness I felt about it.

And then he spoke about his own name, and he gave several different spellings from several different parts of Germany, where his family had lived; and the way he said it, in every subtle nuance of voice, as thick and heavy as he could lay it on, to someone who was tripping on a lot of acid, it was boring.

Old Dr. D.'s old name. Boring old Dr. D.'s old name. Boring old Dr. D.'s old boring old name.

They did some stuff that I didn't know if it was just to freak me out or not, sometimes.

She started feeding the kid. They had broiled a steak, really rare. Then they sliced it. It was about two inches thick, just kind of blackened on the outside. They sliced a very tall, thin slice of it, about a half an inch thick, and laid it over on its side, and then trimmed off the dark parts.

Now maybe I was unreasonable. I keep talking about shell-shocked pacifist vegetarian hippies. But that seemed a tad gross to me, to just give him some raw, warm meat. Took the refrigerator chill off it. Trimmed off the burnt part, and gave him warm, raw meat. But they did meat stuff to me.

She was kind of a neat Jewish lady who came on like some kind of Jewish ladies on television who are fun and hip. Maybe a little Gilda Radnor-ish, except not so crazy. Shorter hair and square. She played tennis a lot, and wore tennis costumes around the house.

I didn't think anything about it until I tripped over there. When I tripped over there, I suddenly was aware that part of what I was in was a hospital room. And she was a nurse. That was one of her qualifications. And he was a hypochondriac. He had a full-race traction bed, a four-poster with pulleys and bags and the works that he slept on—and her tennis costume was just like a nurse's costume, except it had a miniskirt.

There was a little game between them. That game was partly compounded of that he was German and she was Jewish. When I came on and began to see the nuances of the game they were playing between them at that level, I saw that he was a sadist, and she was a masochist. And I wasn't a masochist, and she kept getting me in trouble, and I didn't dig it.

I thought she was my friend, and at one point I about up and split. She showed me such utter contempt that I was shocked. It just blew my mind, how she could have me over and drink with me and talk to me, and have such a low opinion of me.

The only reason I had gotten into this trip in the first place was because I loved her. I had been over smoking dope with her in the afternoon because I loved her.

When I realized that he was doing a thing to me with the lamp, and when I saw that he was running me down the same sentence about Hayakawa again, I had a vision of Hayakawa, from a viewpoint low to the ground, possibly like a small animal. We were in some manicured woods, possibly like a hunting club—and it was San Francisco State College. Hayakawa was wearing a hunting jacket and carrying a shotgun under one arm, and had on a little fedora with a feather in the side— a semi-Tyrol hunting hat, and some kind of jagged black sunglasses; and I was poaching in his hunting club, and he didn't want me in his hunting club. Maybe it was just a totally paranoid vision. He said himself he never knew what to do with me. After I had gone kind of weird and started taking a lot of acid and gotten strange, somebody went to him and pointed out that he had given me straight A's, and wanted to know how come. He never knew what to do with me.

Doctor D. got up and came on as if he and his old lady were from outer space, and they were checking Margaret and me out as examples of not-very-high-level Earth critters, but,

"These ones seem like they might be a little telepathic," and coming on to us very patronizingly like that.

I thought,

He's acting out this scenario in order that he can establish the dominance within this scenario; and if I accept any of this, or any premise of it, I am buying into his movie.

So I just held my hands out to my side and did a big Bronx cheer, and blew us away to another frame of reference.

And he pressed harder and harder to weird me out as I resisted. We tripped intensely for six or eight hours while I was coming on to five hundred mikes of very good acid. I was fighting for sanity and consciousness on my hundredth acid trip, never before having been seriously attacked while I was high, by anyone who knew what he was doing.

I was struggling for my consciousness, running back and forth between,

Is this real? and *Is this not real?*

If I thought it wasn't real, he would do a few things to me to smarten me up, and hip me that it was real. Including some rather wild and weird things to do to someone on acid.

He showed me his cat. He said,

"Poor Mishi is dying. You've got to heal my cat for me, you should heal my cat. Please come look at my poor cat."

We went into his bedroom, and opened the closet door. In the corner of the closet, on the floor, was this cat, looking like it was about to die, its fur all laid down and matted in weird-looking tufts, and sickish looking, cringing, and wouldn't accept food. He had made me watch him cut up raw liver in the kitchen, and he took me in there and offered raw liver to the cat, and the cat wouldn't raise its head, for raw liver.

We walked back into the living room, and we sat down. In a few minutes the cat came walking in out of the bedroom and stood, proud, and beautiful, charged and energized, with every hair standing fluffed straight out and perfect, with a huge aura around it, about six feet, that went into that kind of geometry that the Aztecs put on their idols.

I felt like he had fed me to the cat, and the energy I was looking at on the cat was my energy, that had been fed to the cat. He looked at the cat, smiled fondly, and said,

"Mishi just hates people."

His cat was named Mishi. I don't know if it was a Japanese name, or him and his old lady: Me-She. They were like a hunting team.

I wished I had some grass. His old lady said,

"I know where there's some grass," and went down and gave me a messy newspaper-wrapped bag of about a pound of not-very-good grass. I was trying to get some out to roll a joint, and it turned into this big messy grass scene in D.'s kitchen, which he didn't like, and she tried to talk me into telling him it was my grass, because she didn't want him to think it was her grass. Trying to stick a lie on me at that level, while I was stoned.

He was trying to tell me,

"But you don't understand. The rich people you don't seem to like are the people who preserve everything that is beautiful." And he opened this huge, multi-hundred dollar art book, full of reproductions of everything, sitting on its own walnut and cast-iron stand, and started showing me the beautiful stuff of the world, saying,

"This was rescued by so-and-so, and this was stolen by the Germans and came back to the Louvre," and stuff like that.

He was really into *thing*, seriously bad, and trying to tell

169

me how I didn't pay enough attention to *thing*, and that I was really wrong, that *thing* had to be protected, or there wouldn't be any of this fine *thing*.

He got enthusiastic, and talked, and called me over to him. When I got over to him, I saw two things that were kind of weird. One of them was, as I got next to him, and my vibes became intense to him as I got to within a foot of him, the skin on his face began to look, not like face skin, but like mucus membrane. It got very pink and wet and super-feely, like he was just sitting there *experiencing* me. And at the same time, I saw that he was also so far and deep into experience and sensation that he was combing his hair with a comb and scratching his head, because he had some sort of head rash; and he had scratched this whole head rash into bleeding until he actually, material plane, had his hair combed back and slicked down tight to his head with blood, all over his head, what hair there was.

I'm sitting there tripping with this cat who is this far into sensation and tripped out on it, and rich enough to keep himself out of the crazy. And occasionally he would throw me philosophical questions that were like teaching questions. He asked me,

"Well, what do you see this system to be like? Do you see this to be like an open system or a closed system?"

I was not too swift, and I was thinking of the earth as an ecosystem, and bringing in raw materials from somewhere else and stuff like that, and sort of fliply said,

"A closed system."

When I said that, he grabbed his chair by the arms, and half rose in his chair, and his entire corner of the office, with its black leather office chair, became Nazi-field-marshal-Rommel-in-the-field-looking, and he looked at me and said,

"If it's a closed system, why don't we just eliminate all of you niggers right now?"

I said,

"Oh. I understand. It is an eternally open system, isn't it?

170

There really is no getting rid of anybody or anything. I really see."

At one point he said,

"The way to rule the world is not to be the King or the Emperor or the Pope. The way to rule the world is to control the Evidence Bureau."

I was telling him about telepathic phenomena I had seen, and he was saying he could not admit of any telepathic phenomena unless he had seen them himself. He said,

"Those who control the Evidence Bureau control the admissibility of the evidence; and those who control the admissibility of the evidence control everything."

I realized that he and the professional level of people who were his friends were, in effect, much of the Evidence Bureau.

He continued to try harder and harder to get my head, and he did more and more bizarre things. One little subplot he ran had him and his old lady starting this line of talk like,

"Did the little girl take the pill when you put her to bed?"

And started coming on like they'd done something weird to Dana in the basement, and tried to cop my head about that.

When somebody lays enough suggestion on you like that and you're pretty stoned, you can have a lot of other stuff come up. It got to where a certain very beautiful shade of bright, reddish purple became symbolic of Dana. She had a cape of that color, among other things. And anywhere it was in the room, on the back of a book or as a piece of the color in a painting, became energized and alive-y, and represented her as we talked.

I went downstairs and looked at her and she was fine, and I came back upstairs and said,

"Well, that's enough of that nonsense."

Later on, he got drunker and drunker, and tried harder and harder. While Margaret was standing up, bending over to get something out of her purse on the edge of a chair, he came up behind her, grabbed her from behind, grabbed both her tits, and started humping her, hard—to blow me away some more, again.

While this was going on, I was having some kinds of very personal flashbacks, reliving old stuff, from when I'd had my tonsils out and had been under anesthetic; I was having all kinds of older recorded stuff, way back in the reactive bank, as they say.

It was a ripoff/initiation, depending on how tough you were. If you lose, it was a ripoff; if you win, it was an initiation. You were either the sacrificial lamb, or else you got hip. Take your pick. Left hand path.

When he was doing the hand-held movie camera trip, flicking the switch back and forth, blowing all that consciousness around, from his being in a place where he was really very dominant, I would gather myself together and I would push at him, and try to rise up from how far I was slammed back against my consciousness by what he was doing with his. He would go from really threatening and terrifying to very pitiful, and something that you couldn't possibly come on heavy to—and I would be way over-extended, way over into a sadistic continuum. It was a sadistic/masochistic continuum, and he was sloshing me back and forth on it, turning my strength against me like judo. And it took me a while to figure out what it was, to *attain compassion* and stay in the middle.

As we were sloshing back and forth on that, from me groveling to him groveling, there was this twelve-foot yang and yin sitting on our left sides as if it was hanging on the wall flatwise, suspended from the center. We and it rocked back and forth; and when, at one point that was like a resting point, everything stopped and all the *karma dumbat* stopped, the entire background around both our heads and the whole room as far as you could see in every direction went sky blue with clear space, with heads of saints floating

172

through it. It was so fine and so high that we ceased grappling for a moment, and held our breath as long as we could, and experienced that together. We sort of accidentally erupted to a better place.

We were in what I guess you'd call the *asuras* and the *titan* level, in the eternal struggle of good and evil.

I began to gain control of myself after I was six or eight hours into it. He got up and went to the bathroom, staggered out to go pee again. He'd been drinking quite a bit.

I got my act together while he was gone. When he came back in, I said,

"I'll be leaving now."

And he said,

"Oh, no! Stay for a while!"

*No, thank **you,** baby.*

I split, and we went home. Dana had on some of their kid's pajamas; and I didn't go and see Doctor D. for so long that his old lady came and knocked on the door one time and said she wanted her kid's pajamas back. I didn't have them at the time, and when I went over to give them back and he wasn't home, I threw them in through an open window, and split.

173

Some DMT

MT was one of the kind of things that I never knew anything official about. It came to me completely through the underground. All I knew was underground, and what the underground folks said was,

"They call this the Businessman's Lunch. This is a twenty minute, half-hour psychedelic trip. But you really do it." I thought, *That sounds like fun.*

Some friends of mine had some. I think it was homemade

in somebody's lab. It was pretty brown and cruddy and scabrous looking stuff, wrapped up in a little piece of tinfoil. It didn't look too hot. We put it in an old corncob pipe, and it didn't look as space-age as it was.

They stuck that old corncob in my mouth, and they lit me off. I took a deep breath inhaling drag on it, and I began to accelerate. I began to rush harder and faster, almost, than I had ever rushed in my life. I was instantly transported to a telepathic, magical realm. They had to take the pipe out of my mouth. I couldn't raise my hands up from my lap.

I sat there and looked at these people who were standing around looking at me with humorous, curious and intent expressions, wondering had I got off yet. I could read it across their faces and across their minds as clearly as if they were saying it. As the pipe went around the room, and each one of us took a hit on it as it went around, I watched them turn into the most noble looking, tribal, heavy, elder peyote gods that I had ever seen in my life up to that point, as each one turned on to the pipe.

We sat there and looked at each other as a council of strong, powerful elders.

And then, suddenly, as fast as it had come on, coming down a perfectly perpendicular square-edge drop-off, everything was perfectly ordinary again.

I fell in love with Ina May on DMT. We all toked up on DMT, and I looked at her and just fell telepathically into her, and saw that we just matched up to many decimal places, and were really as telepathic as we could be. It just blew me away. She was with someone else at the time. I looked at it for a second, and I had to put my eyes down, because I couldn't keep looking at it; or I knew I would get so far in that I'd never get back out. I think I did anyway. I think it was too late.

But that kind of thing happened to people. Get stoned with somebody, look at them, fall in love with them, and the whole rest of the material plane doesn't match.

I think the last time I had DMT was with Paul H. over at 69 Harriet Street, which was a warehouse where the Pranksters hung out sometimes, and where various hippies lived at one time or another.

Paul said,

"You want to experience telepathy, this is the stuff. Instant telepathy."

We sat down, and we lit off a pipe each. I looked in Paul's eyes, and every edge, every line, every detail became electric and alive with threads of color running through it, until the entire environment was neon psychedelically pulsingly crawlingly alive and lit. He looked into my eyes and smiled inscrutably, as he lit up the environment, and we played with our DMT.

Then I began to lose it—not quite as square-edged as before; I thought possibly it might not have been as pure, because I lost it slow, and struggled to try to keep it, and felt I had done something wrong as I lost it, until it drifted away and it was gone. After it was gone and I hit bottom, it took me a second or two to forgive myself for ever coming down from it.

I had talked with Patrick G. about dope. He had said he preferred DMT; and I said I thought you had heavier trips and that you were responsible for stuff for a longer time with acid. But Patrick said to me,

"On my last DMT trip, I became a weightless perception floating in space. I enlarged until I became a giant void. Buddha floated in the center of the void, and I floated around the outside of the Buddha and came out of his eye."

I thought, *Well! Pretty complex and stoned for twenty minutes out there, with all this magic.*

Crumbs in the bottom of the DMT pile. See if there's enough to roll a number.

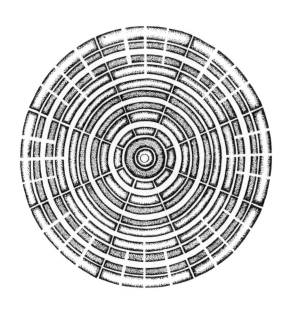

Carrot Tom

eople became known by their most prominent characteristic. Carrot Tom was the only person I ever saw who turned yellow from drinking too much carrot juice. Carrot Tom thought carrot juice was the cure for anything. He drank a *lot* of carrot juice. Carrot juice gives you a pretty good high, too.

I was standing in Stonestown, near San Francisco State, with Carrot Tom and a couple of friends, slugging on a gallon jug of carrot juice, when a cop walked up and asked what we were doing.

We were yukking it up and laughing, slapping our legs, slapping five, and we said,

"Just drinking carrot juice. Here, want some?"

And we held the carrot jug out to the officer. The officer reached for the jug, and just before his hands touched it, it was just as plain as if it said *acid* across his eyes. He became afraid that we were drinking acid-laden carrot juice and that we were trying to dose him. And he froze and jerked his hands back in sheer horror as if we had handed him a spider. We said,

"Oh, come on man, there's nothing in it."

And we all laughed, but he was still uncomfortable in our presence, and walked away.

San Francisco State College Riot

O ne time I went to San Francisco State College to drop acid at the riot. I stood between the commander of the right wing forces of San Francisco State College on one side and the crowd on the other side. The San Francisco Police tactical squad was there, with all of their clubs and mace, standing there in a row at parade rest. I walked out in between them with a lady friend of mine and we smooched. Coming on to this acid, we smooched, and tried to distract everybody from the violence. We were the most interesting thing going on for a while. I think it was her.

It was funny, because San Francisco State College collided with the revolution, and it was like two great ships crashing, and all the spars and thin stuff and superstructure went down on the first encounter.

Summerskill, the president, split to Ethiopia.

Several levels of administration quit or went on vacation or split.

It got down to where the guy who was speaking for the administration was an English teacher from the English department. It had come down to him and he was next.

I saw him standing, looking at a bunch of rioters—hippies, demonstrators, etc.—with his hands on his hips, rolling his shoulders a little macho and threatening, looking like a warlord, strong and heavy and proud. And I thought,

Hoo! Look at this English teacher coming on like this! Where does he get this stuff?

Then I looked and I saw that behind him, down an empty street, with all the cars pulled off of it, in one block, was the tac squad, drawn up into formation, waiting for his call.

There was about two platoons of them in black uniforms and baseball hats and three foot nightsticks—the long ones—all standing at parade rest, like him.

I'd gone in from the far side of the administration building. I knew the back way in from being on the faculty before I had become a hippy. So I was standing at one point inside the building, where two sides of a glass wall jutted out into the crowd, and I could stand out in the middle of the crowd, inside this glass wall—within the circle of the rioters, but inside a glass wall. Looking out to see what was going on, I saw this dude outside.

I went out and saw what he was doing. Then my lady friend and I went out and stood between him and the tac squad. We put our arms around each other, and laid on a long, sweet, passionate smooch right there between the tac

180

squad and the rioters.

I was high on it. It really got me high. It soaked up a lot of juice fast. But I knew I had picked up a ton of karma. And I was running for cover, knowing it was going to come on me fast.

Several people asked for a ride home, and I had several people in the Metro truck.

Up to the top of Twin Peaks, I was okay. Coming down from Twin Peaks, I began to get paranoid.

By the time I got to the bottom of Twin Peaks, coming down across Haight Street, I was getting really bad paranoid, and crazy, and having a hard time driving.

I got to Haight Street. As I pulled across Haight Street after stopping at the stopsign, the vibes got so bad that I thought I had killed someone in the intersection. I thought I had run over someone on Haight Street. I stopped my truck and got out and looked under it, and crawled around, and there wasn't nobody under it.

Talk about people on acid with strange behavior.

I got up, and then I got this sudden feeling that the vibes I had put out had been the telepathic equivalent of screaming, "*Help!*" and I realized I didn't want to attract that attention. I had to say something to let it off. I didn't know what to say. I had nothing to say. I wasn't bright or smart at all. And I thought,

I remember a quotation I read in a spiritual book. I'll just say that, and see if that helps out.

I said,

"Spiritual attainment cannot be bought."

Just as a statement to say, something to stick out in this atmosphere of paranoia. Just to think of that settled it some. It settled me, and I got back in the Metro and fired up and drove on over to this other lady's house.

Parked the Metro out in back, and went in to see my friend, Dee Dee. We used to park our Metro behind her house and use her shower. She was a friend, a real nice lady.

181

I still had residual paranoia on me. We were hanging out, a little weird, not in good shape yet, everything looks a little cheap and tinsely, the television and furniture and stuff all looks cheap and gauche and ugly and tinsely. Margaret comes in wearing red pants and red shirt, eating a salami, and drinking red Kool-Aid. I felt like she was eating me. I was sure she was eating me. I got weirder and weirder, and a lady came in, and she was a nice lady.

She was a nice hippy lady, a Haight Street tripper, who wore her jeans slung down around her hips. She was pretty tough, and she dropped her own acid when she had to. She started coming on to me, and I started sliding paranoid. But it wasn't just paranoid in a way, because I later felt it was prophetic.

I got this vision. Among the people I was looking at was someone who was going to kill me. Every time anyone I was looking at walked as if they were going to go around me, and were going to go out of my field of vision, they were going to step around me, and pull out a pistol and shoot me in the back of the head. I kept having this again and again and again.

This lady would take my cheeks in both her hands, and try to get me to straighten up and pay attention to here and now, try to get me to come off this paranoid trip, and try to get me to settle down and look at her, and know that she loved me, and believe in her, and she would help me. I kept having that vision. I finally got off it after Bobby Kennedy was shot later on.

I felt like the Kennedys were just sacrificed. I could dig Teddy if his courage held out. When he's courageous, I dig him. He said,

"There is no reason for the young people to die for the ineptitude of the old."

God bless him for that.

That trip was very strong. It was on me for a little while, and in more than one location. I walked out of the apartment and went out in the truck and sat by myself in the truck, and I still felt like it. I still had it on me. That was the central thing in my trip for about an hour, that somebody was going to walk around behind me and shoot me in the head.

I don't know about prophecy. There are some things I feel very clearly about; much of what I feel about how the world is being mishandled is agreed upon by hard economists and swamis and yogis alike. That's prophecy to me.

But I just don't know. I have felt foreshadowings of death a couple of times, and known that I was just running right up to the edge of a death. I have felt the aura of the edge of a death.

What I have done whenever I have found that is, I have stopped at that point, and rejected. I don't want to know who. Don't tell me. I'm going to fight anyhow, and I don't want to have any visions to sap my strength. I ain't satisfied that I can't change it. I don't want to be told anything and sit still for it. I don't want to be told anything. I'll mind my own business and fight it.

Entree: Vous

I went to a dinner party one night where the agreement was, I got wasted, and what happened all evening was, I got wasted. There wasn't anything I could do about it, so I went home. It was with Dallas and Jim and Croesus.

Croesus was a dope dealer. He was a bad dope dealer. He was not a nice guy. Weird things happened with him. He would keep dope until the off season and sell it for four times as much. He

184

was a dealer to my friends, Dallas and Jim.

Their trip was far out. They were magicians, and they smoked dope. They smoked good dope, fine dope. They probably took acid and other stuff, too. They were a kinky family. They were a stable set of subconscious who loved each other. He mostly liked guys, and she was very masculine. He was definitely the yinner of the family, and she was definitely the yanger, the stronger of the family. She was Dallas, he was Jim.

Their house was very neat. It was one of those San Francisco works of art. She was an art teacher. There was all this Victorian wallpaper artistically restored, but with these cracks artistically left, and one room being a workshop, which had bandsaws and a plain wooden floor, and lumber stacked around in bins through the room—which was not like the back porch or something. It was the room between the kitchen and the living room. Very arty. The whole house had a lot of unfinished, pretty wood in it, and all kinds of gorgeous, pretty little *things* of every description, little musical instruments and art objects and pictures and old photographs and cameras and old records and record players, Tiffany lamps—the place was just *packed!*

Jim was a craftsman. He had a little piece of ivory he had carved so that it was an amorphous lump at first glance. It was about the size of half your palm, made out of a walrus-tusk or a whale bone or something. Upon looking at it closely, you could see that every bump and every protuberance was the edge of a breast, the piece of a bottom, the curve of a leg, a piece of the belly, just a sensuous, intensely sexual little piece of ivory scrimshaw about four inches long. It was very skillfully hewn. The cat was really a psychedelic artist. He didn't consider himself an artist. Dallas was an artist; he was just a carpenter. He "just did a little carpentry around the house."

They were funny. They loved each other and were a loving couple, the way they were wired. But they were a hunting team. They were one of the couples that seemed to hunt us and court us and hang out with us and spend time with us and do stuff with us. Somehow, we thought we were being hit on.

They would invite me and Margaret over. We would go through these funny trips with them, where we would get stoned with them. They would like to get high with us, because we were trippers and we would get high. They'd smoke dope with us and we'd get pretty stoned. They were pretty clever, smart and fun to trip with.

But at some point, we would go through some heavy *thing* ritual. Because they were deep into *thing*. Weird things went down where I decided to give him a present. I had a little cigarette box which my mother had given me, which at some point while tripping I realized was the most material plane thing I had that connected me the farthest back into the past of anything I had. And I resolved to cut it loose, for that reason.

It was a beautiful thing. I remember it from when I was at a height that when it was sitting on an end table, it was at eye level to me. I remember the match container, which was a flat-black robin with yellow feet and a big red rim on his mouth full of blue-headed kitchen matches, two-color blue head—dark blue body, light blue tip. I remember the lamp, green jade-colored, ornate, dragon, Chinese-y looking lamp putting a bright light down on all that stuff, at eye level to me, however old I was at the time.

So I decided to give it to him. Because they were great hosts, and they were good to us. They fed us *fantastic* meals. Experiences!

I tried to give it to Jim, and he took it and he said,

"Oh, it's beautiful! I'd *love* to have it!"

And then he said,

"But are you sure you want to give it up?" in exactly the right way to make me stop and wonder, did I want to give it up?

186

Then he would say,

"Oh. It's so beautiful! I'd love to have it!"

He caught me by whatever attachment I had to it, and he ran me back and forth with it about this *thing*, until I came to a place of,

Take *it! Just take it, man!*

It blew my mind. Later on, at another point in the trip, we were tripping through an upstairs room, full of interesting things, and there was a horn, a brass kind of hunting horn. I picked it up and blew it, and it had great tone. I thought,

What a great horn!

I was beginning to not like my cow horn from its being so cow, dead, and all—and he saw me like it. And he gave it to me. I didn't exactly carry it around the rest of the day, but I sort of kept it in the room I was in or something, so I would remember it when I left.

Then, just before we were getting ready to leave, he came and told me he had changed his mind, and took it back.

They had a critter called the *slow loris*. It's a primate; it has binocular vision and opposable thumb, and it moves very slowly. In its native habitat, it is frequently invisible from moving so slowly. We all felt that it was telepathic, because it could move so far without you noticing it. It moved one foot at a time—which has always been symbolic of the way I move in heavy times. If it gets really heavy, I move like a slow loris. I put three feet down, and move one foot. Put three feet down, and move one foot.

They had a ring of discolored wallpaper around the top of the wall where the molding was next to the ceiling, all the way around the edge of the room, where the slow loris had peed on the wallpaper while walking around and around the room on the molding.

And *we* believed that the slow loris had the power to cop your mind. That if you got a little spacey around it, it would cop your mind in such a way as that you wouldn't notice it was there. It seemed to do it pretty regular, and we thought that was true. It was not just hippies who thought the slow loris had magical properties, but also the Malaysian natives of its homeland.

One night, me and Margaret were invited to dinner, and who was there but Croesus, a fat, redheaded, freckled, bad boy, about thirty-five years old. He wore a red shirt and black leather vest, a lot of expensive turquoise jewelry, sometimes a squash blossom necklace. He was gross. I have a friend who became a vegetarian because he sat across the table from Croesus at a meal once, and watched Croesus eat a steak in Sam's Original up on Geary Street. This dude was on acid, and he watched Croesus demolish this steak in this red-lit room, and he became a vegetarian that night, and never, ever ate meat again.

We sat there at the dinner table, and got very stoned on some incredible boo which Croesus had brought.

In the course of the evening, I found that I almost never finished a sentence, I almost never finished a story, I almost never finished a thought. I got picked off, ripped off, knocked off every time I opened my mouth. Sometimes I'd find myself coming back in from being spaced out from getting so repeatedly knocked off, and the folks would say,

"Maybe the slow loris got you."

And they proceeded to systematically mess my mind at the dinner table, while we ate an *exquisite* dinner. Beautiful, fresh green peas, lovely vegetables served in beautiful crystal dishes. They had beautiful-vegetarian-dinner, and me, for dinner. Them and Croesus, who apparently had an even stronger understanding between him and them than Margaret and I had between us and them.

I knew at a level that I was being mind-copped. I didn't know what to do about it, and I never got enough juice up to get heavy and do anything about it. I eventually drifted out and split. Me and Margaret got alone outside, and we were hippies again, God bless it!

We ran and laughed and smoked dope and took off and didn't give a hoot and everything was cool because we weren't materialists, God bless it!

But it was good to get the materialist teachings put on you a little bit by some expert materialists—to let you know that the materialists have their experts and their magicians, too. Our relationship pretty much ended when we, at some telepathic level, said,

"No, thank you."

Alienated

 told Margaret one time that I felt like I was an alienated kind of a guy. She argued with me about it, and I said,

"I'm a pretty alienated guy. You don't really know what I'm like."

She said,

"*You* are *not* alienated."

And we let the subject lapse.

A couple of weeks later, she came back to me and said, "I got something I want to talk to you about."

I said, "All right."

"Remember when you said about that you were alienated?"

"Yeah."

"Well, I know this guy who is alienated. And I went out these last couple of weeks, and I've been checking this guy's action out, because I wanted to tell you about where he was really at. This cat's name is Yvars. In the first place, he's a displaced person, and his family is the exiled government of Latvia. This guy sits down in a dark room with no furniture by himself and smokes a lid. He always takes acid by himself in a dark room, and has great confrontations, and sweats and groans and rolls and shouts and has hard trips.

"One time, he got himself into something that got him locked up. When he got locked up, he did fourteen month-long thirty-day shots in solitary for his fourteen months.

"The way he got into solitary was, he hit a guard. When he got out of solitary, the first guard that left himself open enough that he could get a shot at, he would pop him, and they would put him back in solitary for another thirty days. And he did his entire stretch in a series of thirty days at a time in solitary, for popping a guard."

She went on with many more particulars. She had studied this cat's action for two weeks, to have it cold, and to come and lay that on me. She said,

"*You* are not alienated. *This dude* is alienated. *You* are not alienated."

She was right, too.

Angry Goddess

n a second floor apartment in San Francisco with a small family collective, what began as an early evening social acid rap had progressed on to the couples going off to their rooms separately, just to be quiet and alone and trip together.

So Ina May and I were on the mattress on the floor in our room. We were loving, and the vibes were getting very intense. We were both near peaking on some very good acid. While we were loving, I felt that

192

the energy was so high I couldn't contain it anymore, and I was just going to have to let go of the energy. And I realized that letting go of the energy was also going to mean that I was going to come and reach orgasm. I saw that from where we were, from how stoned and how high we were, that I should hold on. But I couldn't.

I let go, and it was grand, for a few seconds.

Ina May was *angry* that I had dropped our energy.

She sprang to her feet on the mattress, and stood there over me, looking beautiful but scary, somewhere between Wonder Woman and Barbarella. She seemed to have an angry, stormy, cloudy sky behind her head, with occasional flashes of bright stars through cracks in the clouds. She looked mythic; and I recognized her as one of the angry incarnations of the goddess.

But I was not really in any condition to be quite so philosophical—because we were very high, and the result of her anger was putting me into a slide, a decline into a very low level of trip where I was actually becoming a little shocky, having clammy sweat and cold skin. My guts turned to water and I had to go into the bathroom. In the bathroom, sitting, almost squatting, knotted up in a ball on the pot with both fists dug deep into the pit of my stomach, I tried to explain to Ina May, while she's still saying,

"What's the matter?"

"Don't you like it?"

"Where's it at?"

"What's wrong with you?"

I tried to explain to her that the reason I am like this is because she is angry. If she could stop doing that to me for a minute, I could get it back together. I was physically ill, as sick as if I had some kind of heavy virus, or was recovering from some kind of heavy jolt. Purely a result of us being that stoned, that close, and turning on to an anger mode.

At a point, she understood me, and was immediately sorry, when she understood how the energy was going.

Then, just as I became ill, I became well. My stomach quit cramping and got solid and felt okay; the cramps in my muscles all opened up; I just relaxed and got back to feeling like I was perfect. And I was.

We went back into the bedroom and began to read the *Whole Earth Catalog*; together. It was near sunrise. We were just leafing through the *Catalog*, and we came across some monkeys, and we realized that *we were monkeys, too.* We looked at each other and had a strong realization of our common ancestry. We could see that the little bits of hair we had sticking around on us were left over from when we used to have hair all over us. When you see with the kind of vision that you can have with acid, you can see one end of the continuum, and project clear to the other end of it. You can see what *this* would be like if it was slid all the way over to *that* end, or what *that* would be like if it was slid all the way over to *this* end. We slid all of our counters back and forth as we looked at each other. We came to where she was much more masculine than I, and I was much more feminine than she. We pushed all my feminine counters over to the end, and pushed all her masculine counters over to the end, and except for the physical part, which seemed unimportant, we could change places and it didn't make any difference.

We talked. We were talking together. It was a very intellectual trip. We were grokking together. We were vibing and having visions together.

At one point, for some reason we didn't understand, we lost it. We didn't know what went on, but suddenly the walls were running in blood, and we were sitting there looking at them run in blood. It was terrible, scary, cold, freaky, chilly, slaughterhouse vibes. We couldn't understand what was going on, and then we realized that we had been incautiously tripping along with the radio on, and the d.j. on the radio had put on a Rolling Stones cut which wasn't nice. It affected our consciousness, and it affected our trip, and it affected our vibes, and it affected our hallucinations until we saw things before we recognized what it was that was causing the change in our trip. When we saw what it was, we turned the radio off and said we had to do something better. That was how we got into the *Whole Earth Catalog*; after the radio had betrayed us we turned to something that seemed to have better vibes.

We were coming to these understandings about continuums and grokkings and that we were only a monkey slid over on one end of the continuum of where a monkey was at, just as Ina May and I were only girls and boys because we were slid over to our ends of the continuum according to the information in our genes. I remember being glad that we were both basically slender—although I was glad that she had a couple of soft places to hold on to. But looking at the whole world, we could see that there wasn't really a lot to go around, and it felt better to not be holding a whole lot of it personally.

When we were thinking about sliding all the counters back and forth, we were looking at a picture in the *Whole Earth Catalog* of the continent of Africa changing into a Coke bottle through a series of fifteen or twenty changes along the way. It became a symbolic picture to us, of that process. I encoded a little piece of it on that picture, and it became one of the nerds in my mind circuits.

We realized we were monkeys, and we were happy we were monkeys. We were delighted that we were monkeys. As soon as the rest of the house and the other folks who were tripping around in various rooms of the house made known that they were ready to come back out and be together in a group again, we all got back together, and that was what we told the group that we thought was heavy: *Man, we're monkeys. That's what we really are, is monkeys.*

Some folks liked it, and some folks were offended by it.

It was kind of funny, because Margaret was one of the ones who was offended by it, and I remember on a later trip, we had a group shared hallucination, if you want to call it that—all four of us were in the same scene with the same scenery going on around us. Michael was very fancy and very colorful, and looked like an old San Francisco Krishna poster with all his qualities and aspects spread in a fan around him, very fancy looking. And across from him, sitting on the couch, is Margaret, eight feet tall sitting down, a gorilla, huge, with long hair, six or eight inches long, all over it. The head was bent down to fit in the room. The knees were sticking up six feet high. She was squatting, using up the whole couch with her butt, sitting there on it, looking at Michael, and loving Michael because he was being so beautiful and had his aspect spread so beautifully.

Ina May and I, observing this scene, saw it as being Hanuman the Monkey God and Krishna. It looked like Margaret was being the incarnation of Hanuman who loved Krishna so much that the monkey became ennobled and is given human intelligence, although a monkey.

Later on, Margaret said she *felt* like a monkey. Not only did she feel like one, she was a male monkey, and she had an erection, and she felt it, and she knows what it feels like. She knows what one of those feels like because she had one, right then.

Talking About Einstein

na May and I were standing in the kitchen, in kind of a loose embrace where we were sort of pressed together in the legs and belly, and then separated apart at the top so we could lean back to a comfortable looking-at-each-other-and-talking distance. We were just standing there braced comfortably against each other, leaning against the wall, **talking about Einstein.** Some of my early grokkings while I was tripping had been on the nature of relativity.

I had had a vision of E=mc², where I understood the mass as a little sphere, and understood the energy as all the points within the mass dissolving apart at the speed of light, if the bonds between them were cut—and that they would be going the speed of light in all directions around the sphere, and although nothing goes faster than the speed of light, we were faced with the speed of light squared to define the sphericity of it.

We were talking about that, and some other aspects of relativity, and developing great, strong, loving rushes that would come right from where our bodies were tight against each other at the pelvis and the stomach, and generate great bursts of electricity that would run up our bodies and reverberate in our skull, hit our mind, and push our mind out where it was easier to understand the relativity, and it was easier to hold the models in our mind while we discussed the matter and energy equation, and the television sets of our mind became very strong and very colorful behind the amount of electricity that was coming up our backbones and going into them. We felt ourselves get smarter, and looked into each other's eyes and loved each other for sharing the understanding that was making us both have these good vibes and this good smart thing happening together. It was very strong, very high. Just standing there stoned, talking about Einstein.

Visions

e were at the Pine Street House, talking and tripping. We hadn't really come on very strong yet, and were sitting around waiting to come on. I was doing these rushes that were so strong that they made a burst of fear come through—it was so strong and so fast and lifted you so heavy that it would give you a burst of fear, as if you felt insecure and were going to let go, and couldn't hold on. There was a feeling that you should hold on, but you

couldn't hold on to it.

Then the rush sort of passed, and I caught another rush. I was trying to take care of it and do it good; and when that rush came, it pushed me into the vision of a Thousand Eyes.

There was a sky-blue matrix that the eyes were set in. It looked like the sky itself, rather than just a flat color. And in between the sky there were eyes put together, in a mosaic— not stylized or painted eyes or anything, but eyes with eyelids and eye sockets, maybe a little piece of face around them, with expressions. Each of the eyes was looking back at me, with recognition, and my entire field of vision was a sphere, so that all I could see was eyes looking back. There were all different kinds and all different colors and all different races of eyes looking back at me.

I've had that vision a couple of times.

There was a yogi on Haight Street who put out a broadside which said,

"If you have had any of these visions, contact..."

Pretty hip. But one of the visions was the Vision of a Thousand Eyes. I thought, *Oh! I've had that one!*

Margaret was always a dramatic tripper. She was tripping on STP one time, and she had a bunch of inner conflicts and ideas that were hanging her up. You could see that it was hanging her up, and that she was caught at a level. She looked self-conscious and her hair looked matted and she was sweaty and having a hard trip. She looked, to my acid vision, as if she had been rolled in something sticky and then rolled in a whole lot of gum wrappers and cigarette butts. It was like somebody who's been in a car wreck, where the car's rolled over a few times and it just takes the contents of the floorboards and sticks them all over you. We were trying to explain to her that she didn't have to be there, and she could change, and that we loved her, and that she could get out of that. We said,

"This is like the gates of hell. And we're trying to help you get out. You can let go and even if you feel like you don't have anything at all, your friends can give you some credit, and with some credit you can run until you feel like you have some again. We are all your friends, and we give you credit to run on."

She understood that. And when she did, it was like she was a helium balloon and someone had snipped the string. She instantly *popped* upwards a couple of levels. As she popped upwards, all the cigarette butts and gum wrappers disappeared and fell off, and she sat up straighter, and her complexion cleared up several shades from darkness back into light and her hair seemed to hang better, prettier and smoother. She got nicer looking and easier in her self, and she opened up and obviously had some level of a *kensho*, or smaller enlightenment, right there in front of us. We watched her have it, and it was instantaneous.

And she had a good rest of the trip.

If your self-concept is like your self is, it makes your self stronger, because they match up together. It's like having all the transparencies lined up right on a printer's color key. Sometimes it's okay to crank your self-concept up just a taste, not in the nature of going on an ego trip, but in the nature of giving yourself enough room to grow into so that you can grow. You have to think well enough of yourself to be able to grow. You can't grow without thinking well of yourself.

Sometimes you can see someone who is trying to grow in

a direction so hard that the self-concept they lay down on top of themselves leads them too far, and it's a little like having the wrong kind of gloss, being a little too glossy, a little too plasticky, where maybe a little matte finish might be more tasteful. You can see somebody whose whole body will look as if it's a little light and polished, shined up a little bit as they try to front themselves out as something that they want other people to think they are.

Also, another person can look at you, and what they lay down on top of you, if it's a lot worse than you are, helps drag you down a little bit; and if it's better than you are, it helps bring you up a little bit; and if it's the same as you are, it strengthens you quite a bit. It can be visual, as well as conceptual.

I learned some of this one night with Margaret. We were playing a game where I was painting up her body with my psychedelic vision, as if my eyes were paintbrushes and I could paint her body, and polish it up. I would do that, and she would cooperate, and there was a transaction of energy taking place between my eyes and her body. We have natural tropisms to look at each other's bodies, and the body sends back information. It's something to look at. It's like looking at television or a movie, rather than like looking at a marble statue.

So we were playing this acid game together, and once in a while she would giggle and become self-conscious and say,

"Oh, no, not little old me."

When she would come on like that, it would be as if somebody had pulled the handle on a chute, and about a half a bushel of potatoes fell down inside her outline, and it would bump her out in a lot of funny lumps all over. It would break through the gloss I had laid on, and wreck it.

I'd say,

"No, no! Don't do that! Don't be self-conscious!" It was like trying to paint her and then trying to get her to hold still long enough for it to dry.

202

That was a kind of healing. And it made both of us more serious, as we realized that we had spent the evening playing with something that was a real healing force, and that we should be more serious how we employed it.

I didn't quit acid because I got scared. I quit acid because I found out it was real, and I was serious. Or it was serious and I was real. All of that.

Once while we were living on the second floor apartment on Pine Street, we went to visit some friends who lived downstairs. They had a nice little altar sort of thing set up in the front room under the window, where they had a nice Tibetan tapestry of some kind hanging on the wall, and they had a little stone Buddha about a foot and a half high, sitting in front of the window.

We went down and and sat quietly together. They knew we were stoned, and it was like you could come down to be with them for a little while, and they understood tripping. It was just dropping in. You didn't have to talk about anything or be social when you were with that kind of people. You didn't have to talk about how the Dodgers were doing or how the weather was, because they knew you had just come to vibe. So you could sit quiet.

We were sitting quiet, and I looked over at the stone Buddha on the table, and it began to change. First the tapestry began to melt and flow a little bit. Then I felt a strong presence of a good spirit. Funny language you have to use when you talk about this, but that's what I felt.

I looked at the stone Buddha, and it became flesh. Not like a little round man sitting there made out of flesh, but each part of it became something very tender and very beautiful from some of us. It was the Buddha with the little helmet with the buttons arranged in rows around the helmet. And every button was a nipple, pink, real, living, beautiful, with texture. And other parts of him were made out of other parts of us, and there was something you could recognize as a piece of a stomach or a piece of thigh, a bit of hair from here, a little something soft and pink from there. He was made out of all our pretty things, all put together into a living mosaic of the prettiest stuff we had, all arrayed onto one little round stone Buddha. It was alive, and it pulsated, and it was as real and alive and flesh as anybody else in the room, for a time. And then it faded, as we lost the vision.

But it held, and we knew that the little stone Buddha was merely a symbol for the telepathic interaction we had shared with a lot of people in a lot of places all at once, and that we had all put out our best and sent out something pretty and received something pretty all over the world, maybe all over the Universe.

I was in one of those places where I was holding ego and I knew it, and I was full of acid and knew the end was imminent. And I was afraid of the people I was with, and didn't want to do it with them, and wanted to do it somewhere else. I finally got in the front seat of my Metro truck which was homelike enough to me that I thought I could do it there. I just curled up there, me and the steering wheel and the speedometer, and let go.

When I let go, I saw time split, *kronon* from *kronon*. I realized about the positive and negative of existence, that you don't have to worry about the negative part because it *ain't*, being its nature.

And in that there was a *kronon* still picture of me here, and then it split apart, and there was nothing in there, and then here was this other *kronon* still picture of me and I was all different. I said, "Wow, this is a new incarnation and that's a past life." I saw myself die and be reborn, and then realized that each one of us dies and is reborn each *kronon*. That's why I'm a believer in the sudden school. It means you can straighten up right now.

Antonio's Birthday

hen we went to Antonio's Birthday Party, we were living on Pine Street, Michael and Margaret and Ina May and I. We decided to go out to Antonio's birthday party, which was sort of a social event, because he was an astral magician, and he would probably have a bunch of magicians come to his party. It sounded like it would be fun. Although some people were shocked that I would go to Antonio's birthday party at all.

206

I remember one time I was in the back yard behind the Family Dog. There was a big, tight circle of about fifty or sixty folks, several layers deep, smoking dope. I was standing in that circle, and somebody just came along and threw a body block in the middle of my back, and jolted me. I turned around just in time to see Antonio disappear out through the crowd.

While he burrowed into the crowd, I backed out to the edge of the crowd, and ran, hot, around to the other side of it. When he came out the other side, I struck at him like a fencer, and put my index finger in his belly button.

It made him have to jump, and suck his guts up, and he says,

"My *chi!*"

And I said,

"No, man, *my* chi! I'm getting it back. The one you took from me on the other side of the crowd!"

I wouldn't *do* that to somebody who wasn't a magician, who knew what they did and was doing it on purpose. You may not be able to stop crime, but you *can* do something about how well it pays.

Antonio could be charming when he was stoned. He had a big mop of hair. We worked out a bunch. And he worked out with me, too. We were always going to straighten each other.

I remember one night when I was drinking beer with him in the lobby of the Straight Theater, when Rockin' Jody walked up behind me and said,

"Drinking *beer* with *Antonio! In the lobby of the Straight Theater?!!*"

Antonio was wearing no shirt, and one of those Indian vests with the little mirrors embroidered into it, a real short skimpy vest, a big mop of hair, and a great big, fancy, drawn-on caste mark. Hindus put a mark on them that indicates their caste. Tony would put one on that was all drawn up fancy so it looked like a jewel. And he would hold yoga classes during the break at Monday Night Class.

He could do all the hatha yoga positions real easily—so could Margaret—and for a while he used to go around in a cossack outfit, with real wide pants and boots that came up to mid-calf—just very dramatic costuming all the time. There was a thing he did to me one time: it was as if he psychically struck a pose. He knew how to strike a pose physically very well—a lot of what *Tai-Chi* is about is learning to strike a pose, and then try to bring yourself to the head place that goes along with that pose. Learn how to strike a noble pose, and then try to bring yourself to a noble frame of mind to go with it.

He struck a pose and he looked like a Buddha—except out of the corner of his eye, where part of him was saying,

"How'm I doin'? How'm I doin'?"

We dressed up in our party-going best, and we had a mirror that was a little Navy flyer's signalling mirror, with a little cross on it and directions on the back about how you could signal a plane with it. It was very accurate; there is an aiming system where the shadow of the mirror falls on your hand, and the cross hole in the mirror falls on your hand, too. When those two are lined up, it was aimed, and you could aim it thirty or forty miles that way. We used that mirror to lay out some lines of THC for us to snort. We laid out a line for Ina May and she snorted it, and one for Michael, and me, and Margaret, and we took off for the party. On the way to the party, we found out that there had been a slight error, which was that Michael hadn't snorted THC with the rest of us; he had snorted a cap of acid that was mixed in with the THC, and he was beginning to come on seriously dynamite from snorting this cap of acid. He didn't have much to say; we just sort of led him around for the evening. He'd occasionally say,

"Wow," or

"Far out!" or something like that, but we mostly led him around, having him sit here, wait here, we'll be right back, come this way,...

We went over to Antonio's house. He and his roommates had several floors of the same house. When we came in, we were greeted by one of the disciples of the Ashoke Fakir. In fact, he was the one who would sit over beside the Shoke and mix the caste mark that the Shoke would use. He was the one I had seen messing over the Shoke again and again at the chanting ceremonies. He opened the door and smiled. He had a pair of teeth that stuck down over the corners of his mouth like fangs. Maybe he was having some dental problem. But somehow or other, he had fangs.

The first room we walked past, we looked in. It was a bare room with nothing in it. The walls were blue, and there was a hundred-watt light bulb hanging from the ceiling on a wire with a pullchain on it. On one of the walls was a dartboard target. There was a guy in the room throwing darts at the target.

He had that wild, peeled, scalded, boiling look of someone who has just shot up on Methedrine. His eyes were very openy and wet, and he looked like the cover of the old Zap comics.

He was dropping the darts in the middle of the bull's eye. Zap, one after another, right in the middle.

He looked up as we walked into the room and he said,
"You want to play darts?"
And we watched him hit a couple more. *Whap!*
And he hit a couple more. *Whap! Whap!*
We thought,
Ahh. There is more to this than meets the eye. This dude is into his thing, and willing to bet his ego on it.
He would bet his ego on beating you, and if you played with him, you'd be betting with your ego; and it was dangerous to even play. It was dangerous to accept the challenge.
We smiled and said,
"No, no, you look like you're pretty good there." And

stepped out of the room and continued down the hall.

This dude had it *down* about throwing darts in that room.

We went up a floor and went into the living room on the next floor. As we walked in, T.K. and Jenny were there. T.K. and Jenny were a funny pair. Jenny was a big, young, pretty girl, and T.K. was a little bit older, being a little grey. He was blind, or almost blind. He could just see enough to get around a little bit. And T.K. was a stoner.

When I came in, I hadn't noticed at first, but there was a hi-fi stereo set sitting on the floor beside T.K.'s chair. And both speakers were sitting on the back of the chair behind his head. As I walked in I looked at him and said,

"T.K.!'

And I wasn't trying to show off or anything. I just revved up a little bit because I liked T.K., and I vibed with him. I had a feeling with him.

And T.K. says, sarcastically,

"Aw, look. Stephen's *vibrating.*"

I felt a little put off that he had said that in that way, and I looked at him to see where he was at, and why he was coming on to me so funny. Then it looked to me like he turned the hi-fi set on real loud. But there was no record on it. Just a faint hum coming from behind his head in both those speakers. And he put his juice behind that electric juice coming out of the wall. He vibed augmented, electronically. It was sort of strong, and pretty overpowering, because there was a lot of strong signal coming out of those speakers, although there was no sound. And I jumped on with him. Rather than hassle with him about the juice, I jumped on with him like jumping up in his lap, and jumped on the rush with him.

We rode the rush together, and all of a sudden, we peaked at the top and we got very stoned together. And T.K. said,

"Now, I told you I was the wizard of Naz around here."

I felt that he *was* a wizard.

I said good evening and cut loose, and went on upstairs to

the next floor. Antonio was around the house, graceful and beautiful, looking somewhere between a vicious street waif Haight Street hippy and Jackie Onassis.

We went into the top attic room in the house, and there was a little altar there. The guy who managed the altar was the guy who had let us in, with the fangs. And we saw that this was not an altar to be hanging out at. This guy made a mockery of the other altar where he worked part-time. In fact, he had an altar here in this room, just for the purpose of making mockery. And we turned and left, not wanting to be part of making mockery that way.

As we came back downstairs into the next room, we came out of a door and Jody was standing there. And he said,

"Ha-ha-ha, hee-hee-hee! I sure am glad I didn't take a couple of caps of acid just in case I might run into you over here, he he he!"

And I realized that he *had* taken some caps of acid, who knows how much.

He went for me, and started overpowering me with his presence. He began to blot out the reality I was seeing with another overlaid reality, *and did so.* He completely blanketed my sensorium with sheer output—except for my left hand, where I was holding hands with Ina May. I squeezed her hand, and she squeezed back, and I saw that even with my sensorium blanketed, I was cool, unique, alone, safe; and as I realized that, his manifestation melted back until the room was more easily accessible to all entities, and we began to leave without having to say where we were going.

We started down the stairs, and Jody began to holler as we were going down the stairs,

"Hey! I got a connection for a guy that can get kilos of gold. Kilos of gold! *Kilos of gold!!* **Kilos of gold!! Kilos of gold!!! KILOS OF GOLD!!!**"

Jody hollered it down the stairway as we went all the way downstairs: Kilos of gold.

He finally said,

"Where are you going?"

I said, "We're going to go to the Carousel to hear the Grateful Dead."

And when we got to the Carousel and went in, Patrick G.'s old lady was there, as if she'd been waiting for us.

She looked at me and said, "Oh! You've come at last!"

She took me by the hand and led me quickly through the lobby and over to a corner of the dance hall, where Patrick was standing, with an angry power-magician vibe on, stalking around the back in the middle of the Carousel. The Grateful Dead sounded real small, and looked real tiny, way at the other end of the room, and you could hardly pay any attention to them. Within fifteen feet of Patrick was a couple hassling, a fist-fight breaking out, somebody setting a wastebasket on fire, and stuff going on like that, right in his immediate vicinity, just violent anarchy and breakdown happening for a fifteen-foot circle around him, with him standing in the middle like the Sorcerer's Apprentice in *Fantasia*, directing it.

I came in, and I saw that, and I made this instant decision on how to do something astral and telepathic, which I've never done before, and have no plan of ever doing again. I looked at him and I said,

"Patrick!"

And he looked at me. When he looked at me, his juice just *flowed* to me. I established that connection. He had all the energy in the hall pretty much balled up in that little bunch of fights in the back of the room; it was maybe three thousand people there, with about a thousand of them on acid. This was one of the times when I've felt a foot-wide tube of energy come off somebody, and it flowed to me really fast. And at the same time that it flowed to me, I mirrored it and redirected it to Garcia. As I did, it was just like having a volume knob on the Grateful Dead. They just started to roar, and took off about fifteen foot tall, filled up the room and were an overpowering presence in the room, which after all is their natural habitat, and where it's really at when the Grateful Dead are in concert.

Patrick & I & Me

Patrick M., or Patrick-and-I, as he called himself, slept in the street and in corners and in doorways, and wore this sweat shirt with the hood up all winter long; and when it came into the spring, and he took that hood off, his hair was in a knot, that was more-or-less on top of his head.** But like a few other guys that I knew, his vision of himself made him think that his haircut was symmetrical, somehow; and although it was a knot with a couple of crazy loops to the ordinary vision of the civilian on the street, in Patrick's self-concept, it was a huge natural, with gigantic six-inch curls, and covered his head with a huge bushel of hair. In his self-concept, he was royal, and he was got up just royally—although in the material plane, it was just overalls and a grey sweatshirt with a hood.

Patrick was one of the folks who was best at looking like royalty. He assumed the mudra, or posture, of pride so well that he looked like an emperor, or a prince.

The way I met Patrick in the first place was when I was doing Monday Night Class at the Straight Theater on Haight Street. Patrick would come in and refer to "Patrick and I" all the time. At several points, I wanted to ask him where was the other guy, where was Patrick, and then I realized that *he* was Patrick. And I. Both.

He would be into my juice just as hard as he could. But he would come to every meeting. He would do things like walking through the crowd, muttering phrases and sentences and exclamations and cussings and weird things, just a steady running spark of weird jive, changing variety all the time. If he would hit on anything that would zing anybody's subconscious and attract their attention, he would switch to that channel and come up on them with a bunch of that. And just peel them in their tracks.

He was a telepathic shark, cruising through town. He would do various kinds of things. If it was a sexual cuss of some kind that weirded somebody out, they'd just get a lot of that. People who were weirded out by crazy talk, he'd just come over and really talk crazy on you. Whatever got you. Mobile. He was, like Doctor D. says,

"Instead of looking at somebody as being a failure of some sort, look at how good they are at what they do."

He had been living in my car across the street, our old Metro van. We'd moved out of it when we moved into the apartment. The left front tire was flat, and it took me a long time, and two trips to go buy jacks, and several trips to get that tire jacked up, and it was funny because it left the van perfectly flat, and he was sleeping in it. I halfway felt like he

215

was influencing me there. I don't really believe that, but it was a paranoia of the time, that you always had to check all that stuff out.

I saw that he was not doing well. He was peeing in a milk carton and not eating anything, just hanging out inside there, vegetating, in some kind of a deep funk. Who knows what he may have taken. He had been a juvenile delinquent since he was nine, and was a Haight Street kid on Haight Street, and he didn't read no Aldous Huxley about whether he should take acid or not.

I finally ejected him from the van. He walked directly across the street into the basement of our house. He walked in to where there was a cot in the basement, lay down on it, and resumed his posture.

I came down with a plate of food, and gave it to him. I went down later on, and the plate of food was crusted over and untouched. He wouldn't eat, and was lying there.

We were upstairs peaking. The four grownups were banged on acid and laying on the bed at the Pine Street house, just laying there in a heap, our bodies at ease and our minds mixing together, sort of above us.

At times like that, I remember very clearly Margaret and I getting out of our bodies and floating up about four feet above the bed and looking back down at our bodies together, me and her being telepathic and experiencing astral projection together. Two kinds of ESP at once, telepathy and astral projection. That's an interesting thing about ESP—people talk about different things of it as if it were separate compartments; but it's not, really.

Patrick picked the lock on the back door, came down the hall, and stepped into the doorway of the room where we were all four on the bed, completely wide open.

He looked at us and did a *mudra* or gesture of
I have a good reason for being here.
Then he switched to a different *mudra* of,
It's okay. It's only me.

And switched to a different *mudra* of,
Don't get up.
And switched to a different *mudra* of,
Don't get up, I'll leave anyway.
And switched to a different *mudra* of,
I just got here. What's going on?.
And switched to a different *mudra*.

And each one of them stopped us from moving while we paid attention to what it was; and before it could come to any fruition where we could make a decision and *do* anything, it changed to a different one. He stood there and flashed them at us, several a second, for some minutes. And stood there in the meantime with his great big old hungry astral eye out, just sucking us up, peaking there.

I finally got enough moxie to get up. There was a spell being put upon us. I took him by the hand, and led him to the back door, stepped him out the back door, locked the back door better so he couldn't pick it,... and came back and lay down again. We integrated ourselves and got our juice back together and healed up the big old hole that was there.

It wasn't that we were stingy and he couldn't have none. But he was unclean, from where he was at. Very hard to be around while you were stoned—and he knew it. That's why he did it. That was his magic.

Later on, he got up and went out in back and peed on a box of puppies that were out in the back yard. It was a statement, just a pure statement.

So I thought, *Patrick, you have got to go.*

We had these two big zip-together sleeping bags that belonged to my brother-in-law. I was in one of those places where I didn't know who belonged to what, this was the equipment I needed at the time. I snatched up one of the sleeping bags, and went downstairs. I said,

"Patrick, you are going to have to split."

I came on to him forceful, and he went pitiful. And when

he did, he took me off again. And my energy flowed from me to him, and I was in a completely double level of mind. On one mind, he had just judoed me, tricked me, and was mugging me in the basement, ripping me off for my juice which was flowing in a foot-thick tube of hot yellow white vibes between me and him, running off of me into him; and at the same time, my mind was thinking, *Get a good hit; you'll need it for the road*. It was a ripoff/transfusion. Involuntary and voluntary at once, as it is easy to be on something like that.

I took him by the hand and led him out to the front porch, and we stopped on the front porch steps and I put the sleeping bag in his hand. He had ten dollars that he had gotten from somewhere, and I started to tell him something about where he was at, and I looked at him and he was not listening to me the least speck. He was looking down the block, about four blocks down the road. He was on the road already, and I was already in the distant past. He was already looking forwards to new frontiers. And I knew it was going to be cool. I just gave him a pat on the back and sent him off with the sleeping bag.

Later on, when my brother-in-law found that we had given his sleeping bag away to this crazy in the basement, it was part of a family feud that went on until I went downtown and bought a new pair of twin sleeping bags and gave them to him.

Patrick would come right up and sit beside me on stage, just a little behind me, and he would lean forward, and put his mouth up to my ear and talk to me so low that only I could hear him. And while I was talking to Monday Night Class about whatever I was talking about, he would start coming on with,

"You know, of course, that when you step out the stage door tonight, and step out into the alley, I'm going to get you. I'm going to be waiting for you outside when you come out tonight, and I'm going to get you."

He wasn't going to get me. I have never heard of him

hurting anyone. Usually he was painfully compassionate. Some of the craziest places he got were, that you weren't supposed to break the skin law. He said that when a kid gets slapped for biting the tit, that's the skin law; you aren't supposed to break the skin law. It's okay to eat things, but you aren't supposed to break their skin. He would swallow his rice whole. I would say,

"Patrick, you got to bite your rice. It ain't as good for you if you don't bite your rice. You got to bite your rice."

And Patrick would argue. He was such a shell-shocked, emotionally blown pacifist that he didn't want to bite his rice.

The Synapse Dance

here was one trip at the Synapse dance in San Francisco, where I got dosed with PCP—twice. I got hit once and didn't like it, and went looking for some acid, and asked for acid and got hit again with more PCP. And I got *very down,* on PCP, wandering around this place.

Ina May was on acid; and I could see her moving through the crowd. She had a *beautiful* aura—guys would turn and snap to attention as she went by. And I couldn't feel her. I was all downed out and couldn't feel anything. I was disconnected from her for about half the evening.

That was the night it got weird on stage. The room was supposed to be a bunch of San Francisco's most *vibratory* people, thousands of them, invited to this one big bash with the Grateful Dead, to make some vibes happen at the Carousel. And we were all there.

I blew my cow horn to start the meeting, and we started it off pretty stoned and it went on pretty stoned and pretty active.

I was standing beside the left side of the stage, talking to a guy with a great, big red, white, and blue eagle on the back of his vest, a piece of commercial equipment, not something hand-made—he was obviously some rich cat who was trying to go like a hippy—and he got *mad*. He'd had a fight with Bill Graham, and he got quite mad. He started really bitching up a storm about this fight he'd had with Graham; and I thought we ought to be *cool, man*. There's three or four thousand stoned people in this room, and the Dead is blowing hard.

I took his uptightness, and thought,

"Well, Garcia's got the largest machine for integrating in the room, with the Dead up there onstage, so I'll throw it to Garcia and see if the Dead'll just chew through it like the old Coke bottles in the garbage disposal."

I did that, and at that instant, Garcia broke a string. He broke a string and he couldn't go on without it, it was too vital. He called the band to a stop, and went in the back and started getting his strings back together.

As he went backstage and started putting his string together, the hall started falling to *pieces*. The vibes started turning sour. People started getting weirded out, competitive, a whole bunch of folks got up on the stage. I'd been hanging out up on the stage—I guess I was into the juice, too—everybody there was into the juice in a sense.

People onstage started getting pretty obstreperous, and

this guy started taking off his clothes, and this lady took off *her* clothes, and this other guy gets up on stage and says,

"Ah-haa! We have *Eve*. And we have *Adam* here," and all that kind of stuff. And then he says,

"But *I* saw her first." Just cuts a dichotomy with the full juice, at that speed.

Then the vibes started getting *weird*. Stuff started getting stranger. People were climbing on the stage and taking their clothes off. One guy was climbing the sound tower, trying to evoke John Finlay, who was supposed to be on the East coast. He says,

"*Johnn Finlayyy!* I know you're out there somewherrre!"

Trying to evoke his presence in the hall. Magicians, helping each other out, coast to coast.

Dana was there, and Margaret, so I had them hang out behind the amps. Leary was there behind the amps to stay out of trouble. Women and kids and Tim Leary behind the amps.

Now I didn't exactly trust how this jam was going to come out. The only reason I'd done the thing about blowing my horn at the beginning was that I'd thought,

"Well, at least if I blow my horn in the beginning, I will have introduced myself and the horn to all these people; and at some point later on in the jam, I might have to use it as a tool."

It was like activating my tool, to use it at first like that, even though it gave me a certain amount of responsibility for a bunch of jive that might go down. It's double-edged that way.

I went up to Garcia, showed him my horn, and said,

"Do you mind if I go up on the front of the stage and blow this horn off your stage?"

He says,

"Man, it's up for grabs. You can do anything you want."

So I started up for the front of the stage. By the time I got to the front of the stage this time, it was just wall-to-wall packed with people into the juice, all trying to get the juice. And Don H., from Harbinger, tried to do something. I looked over and I saw that he was getting a certain amount of juice from what he was doing, and I thought,

"I'm just going to short-circuit that so-and-so. I am just going to take this juice and channel it out of this thing that is going on, and direct it into something else."

I went over and I put my left hand on top of his head, which was quite bald. Excellent contact. I just slapped my old, sweaty hand down on top of his head, and started sucking his juice off as hard as I could suck it; and he was so crowded in among people that he couldn't even get his hands up to take my hand off his head.

I took my horn in the other hand, and started blowing my horn, and taking all that crazy juice on the stage and just sucking it up and blowing it right out through that horn—*Whaaaaaooooooooooooooooommmmmmmmmmmm!*

Now, there were about five or eight hundred people out in the audience who were a bunch of old OM-ers, and they all picked up the OM, and the other people who had heard me blow at the beginning picked up the OM.

This meeting was sliding into randomness very fast, and that OM just caught it like a catcher's mitt. We went into that big OM, three thousand people OM-ing. They picked it up, and the vibes went up *high*, man. And it transcended.

It was the people on the floor who did it, because the people on the stage were into the juice. But the people on the floor all OM-ed, and picked that vibe up, and the people claimed the territory and claimed the vibe, and made it be a good scene, and Garcia got his string fixed and came out to the front of the stage; and as soon as he started playing, the people started melting off the stage, and we took off *Whsssh!* Full sail. Living thunder on the move.

When I went onstage to blow my horn to start the jam, Rockin' Jody Morningstar came by and was standing at the stage, chatting with me. And while he was there, Joe came

223

walking by, and saw me on the stage. He looked at Rockin'
Jody, and said,

"Is the eagle gonna fly tonight?"

And Rockin' Jody says,

"Yeah."

But I went into it knowing,

*Somewhere in the course of this evening, this thing is liable to turn
bad; and if it does, the most useful thing I can have is a non-electronic
way of reaching the room.*

That's what I liked about my cow horn. I could hit the
whole room as hard as an electric guitar. And it was
organic; they couldn't pull my plug.

We were juice mechanics. We really played a lot of stuff
like that.

That was the first time I ever saw Tim Leary put the
social-position freeze on somebody. He put it on me. Later
on, I saw him put it on somebody else, and I understood
what it was.

I was talking to him enthusiastically, and I laid my hand
on his arm while I was talking to him.

He just stopped, and looked down at my hand. He kept
looking at it until I ran down, looked to see what he was
looking at, and let go of it.

Later on some of us went into the Performers' Room, a
room about eight-by-ten feet. When we walked into the
room, we didn't see anything that attracted our attention at
first, except a low table with something on it. There was a
door, which we thought led to another room because there
was nobody in the Performers' Room. We went over and
opened one of the doors, and it was a closet, and there were
two speed freaks shooting up in the closet. They came
walking out past us. We looked around, and there was a guy
who had come in and lost something on the floor. He was
crawling around on his hands and knees, cursing and
fumbling in his search, in front of this table that had a
golden-colored lead toad on it, and some trash scattered

around on it. That kind of altar has random stuff randomly scattered, rather than neat stuff neatly arranged.

I looked over and this guy was laying on the floor in the corner, got-up in hippy clothes, looking really revolting. His hippy clothes had a buckskin leather gusset in the crotch, which was stained many colors. He was laying there with his legs open, revolting looking. We looked at him, and felt revolted, and he writhed in pleasure from it. We realized that that was his bag, being revolting, and he got off when folks thought he was revolting.

We left that room and that altar quickly, as we discovered what kind of church was being served there.

Tam

One day, Michael, Ina May, Margaret and I took off from the City in our old Metro truck. We walked back up a creekbed on Mount Tamalpais.

The way we got the Metro truck was, we were living in an apartment, with Margaret working, and Margaret said,

"I can't work no more. I can't stand it. It's payday and I want to quit. I've got $186 for two weeks work. We could either use that for next month's rent and groceries, or we could buy a truck. I don't want to work any more. Let's buy a truck."

We went out and searched and searched, and found this old Metro truck that was all banged up on one corner, and the front wheels were six inches to the right of the rear wheels—but it tracked perfectly. You could go seventy miles an hour straight down a hill, and it would track perfectly. Just had one set of wheels over to the right a little.

We did a cosmetic job on it. We patched up the broken-off, crunched up fender with paper and tape, and painted it with spray cans until it looked like it was fixed, but was just cardboard. We did a paint job on it to make it look like a mail truck or something, so nobody would notice it, and moved into it.

We drove the old Metro over to Mount Tam, and dropped, and walked up the hill back up into a meadow.

We used to carry horns with us to blow, as a yoga. I blew horn a lot, and a bunch of other people got horns because they thought it was a good yoga; and they did that with me, sometimes. We would blow together and listen to the harmonics. It was like om-ing.

One of us had a horn that was made out of a piece of seaweed that had been plasticized; two of us had conch shells, and I had my old cow horn.

I wanted them to blow horn to *shape up.* They'd been on long enough that they'd come on pretty good, but they were still a little crusty and not real high-looking to me. I wanted them to look higher.

Margaret didn't know how to blow horn at all. I said,

"Okay, you guys blow horn and I'll help you get it together so you can blow."

I stood over about twenty feet and said,

"Blow!"

Margaret picked up her horn, and blew this real, weird squawk on it. It was so weird, and so vile that it caused me to instantly bend over from the waist in an L, and barf. Two movements: it hit me in the stomach, I bent over and barfed.

I said,

"No, no! Not that way!" And I told them how to blow.

As they blew, you could see crusts, that looked like accretions, snot or calluses, or crust of some kind, that was over their auras, and made their auras look dull.

As they blew, that stuff melted away, and they became pretty psychedelic hippies right before my eyes.

After all that horn blowing, we just tripped around the mountaintop, having a really good time.

I was laying down on the ground, tripped out into the dirt—as you could be when you let your vision go to the very smallest things in front of you: dust motes, the gravel and stuff—letting myself flow into the mountain.

I felt myself become one with the mountain.

I felt myself become one with everything that was alive on the mountain.

I became so one with the mountain that I knew that I was them and they were me, and I wanted my friends to feel what I could feel, I wanted them to understand this, too.

I went over to where they were, and they were tripping along and talking a little bit.

I said,

"Listen. Be quiet, and listen *now*."

At that moment, all the animals and all the birds, all the bugs and rabbits and critters on the whole mountaintop, all made their noise at the same time. Not loud, but a giant, huge sound, coming up from acres and acres and acres at once. Every creature there made its sound. And we all heard those creatures make that sound to us and tell us that we were all really one. We were one with them and we were one with the hill. We were all really One.

I heard years later that the Indians say that God's Name is the cry of all the animals at once.

We felt like something as strong as that was a new beginning of some kind. We came down the hill, and the

228

creekbed, which had been almost dry when we went up, was running bank-full of clear water as we came back down.

We stopped, and each one of us took a little of the mountain's water out of the creek and poured it on us. It was like a little baptism from the earth.

We went back down the mountain, and we were so changed by that that it made a tremendous change in our living. We went home and we saw that some of the stuff we had around was not nice. We had an amusing picture on the wall, a picture of some kind of home for some kind of ladies who needed a home. They were tall and skinny, short and fat, weird looking in one shape or another, and it was a funny picture. But when we came down off the mountain and looked at it, it was not a funny picture. It wasn't funny at all. It was gross to have it on the wall to laugh at, and we had to take it down.

In another room, we had some rubbings from some foreign country, where someone had taken this beautiful, white, soft paper and laid it down over some old carvings, and rubbed on it, and made rubbings. So we had these pretty rubbings on the wall. When we looked at the pretty rubbings, we saw that they were pictures of soldiers with spears and swords herding slaves on a chain. And we saw that we didn't like it. It had no artistic value, actually, as a thing. If it had been part of a true story, it might have been different. But as an artifact, as a piece of art up on the wall,...there was a lot of stuff like that which, when we looked at it, just looked gross. And we took it down. We couldn't hack it.

It was like a search for some kind of astral purity. When you're stoned, every little thing resonates so hard that anything that's actually a little gross is pretty strong.

That was really a seminal trip, for all of us. It put us into a oneness and a compassion so we couldn't take any joy in people being hurt, or representations of the creatures in tortured fashions. It wasn't good to look at.

For exactly the same reason, I don't like a picture of a Christ on a crucifix with nails in him. It's a mistaken symbol. He should be pictured alive, and joyful.

The Great Harbinger Bust

here were big collectives started all over the Bay Area. We started hearing that there was this *great big* collective, several hundred people on sixteen hundred acres. It was up at Harbin Hot Springs. They had a hot bath, medium hot pool, swimming pool, hundred room hotel, machine shop, wood shop, auto shop, photography studio, chemistry lab, library with all the back issues of scientific magazines back to 1900 in several different fields—tons and tons of *thing*.

And it got run right down through the ground, all out, gone, kaput, finished, used up, until the last time I went up there, the windows were shot out of the hotel, there was nobody living there, there was a car body dragged across the road shot full of holes, saying "Welcome" and a bunch of bullet holes all through the welcome sign.

It was an umpty-ump hundred thousand dollar trip, went crash, down the tubes. A lot of money in the movement has been tied up in a bunch of bullshit; that was some of it.

It took eight months.

It sounded like a real thing. We went up to see it, Harbinger hot springs. It was the first big collective we saw, and we got to see how it worked a little bit.

All the speed freaks and power trippers used to go up there and play *King for a Day*.

We came up there the first time, and we drove through a lot of that pretty northern California stuff, pretty golden hillsides with little patches of trees that looked like the cork oaks in Spain—beautiful country up there north of San Francisco—thinking, *How beautiful it would be to live out here in this kind of place. Boy, wow!*

Then we got to, *This is the edge of their property. Wow! You mean we're on their property now and from here all the way back, going on and on and on, . . . Look! This is larger than many apartments! Larger than many apartments at once!* We were city people.

We came charging up the hill, and got about halfway up toward the place, and there were these two big thrones by the road. There was a pair of nice young hippies, a guy and a girl, and they had these big thrones, eight feet high up the back of them, with big arms, and decorated up like thrones. The couple was wearing crowns, and were all done up like royalty. They had told them they were the king and the queen. Talk about being sent up in a box kite. They didn't have no juice, no authority, no say-so. They just had those thrones and those crowns, and all the speed freaks who came by would just take a bite.

By the time we got to them, they had been peeled. The poor babies had really been hit on a lot. They had been run over a bunch. They saw us come up and they said,

"Man, there have been a *lot* of tough people, a lot of speed freaks and heavy trippers go past this here place, and we're really glad you're here. We really hope you can do something up there to help it out."

They were really glad to see us, and we felt somewhat sorry for them that this funny organizational system had put them in an untenable position.

We went on up the hill, and when we got there, it was like they said—just *everything* going on. Ina May remembers a lady in particular who wasn't wearing anything but her skin and a wolf skin, with a head open above her head, and the jaw open with all its teeth, a wolf pelt down her back. It went from that range to full-dress regal getup, which some folks were into in those days.

But it was too loose to do anything with. We couldn't do anything with it. We had opinions about it, but there was nothing we could do. We went a few weekends. The last time we were up there, a car was dragged across the road, with bullet holes shot in it. The place had folded up. The buildings were about half destroyed. The water had quit coming hot to the hot springs; they never knew who they got mad to cause *that* to happen.

The place had to lay empty for years for the local people to forgive and forget the scene that was thrown down on them. Just a completely loose bunch of hippies on the weekends out there to do their number.

It was the weekend visitor party scene for San Francisco; and it got hundreds and hundreds of visitors every weekend who just came and partied their brains out on them. Although it hadn't been spoken yet, some of it was the early days of boogie till you puke.

The people who were holding it together were very few in number, and very hard pushed to try to hold this thing together, because it was so loose. It would expand up to a whole lot of people who didn't care very much, and it would shrink down to a very few when the bill paying was due.

They didn't really have any means of production. They had a car shop, but it was just for maintaining their cars. All the stuff they had was only for maintaining; they had no means of production whatsoever, except that they always thought that one of their bands was going to hit like the Beatles and make them millions. That was Plan A.

Their Plan B was to keep having a sufficient number of people come and join and throw all their stuff in the pot, to keep making it that way. It lasted about eight months. Without having a means of production, without being independent, that was as far as they could run, was about eight months. They cycled several hundreds of thousands of dollars, and blew up in about eight months on hepatitis, overflow sewage systems, injunctions from the county about overcrowding and how they're handling their water and their sewage, and their people dealing to the degree where the heat was down on them.

H. had a good, sentimental rap. But his rap was that he was Jesus returned, and I don't know how he got a bunch of spacey hippies to go along with him for that. That was the real thing wrong with H., was that he came on like he was Jesus. Nobody believed it, but it was a neat place to hang out. So they copped to it. The place was built on a lie. That was the lie it was built on, that folks copped that he was the returned Jesus.

H. was a funny kind of a magician. A great, big, six foot two, two hundred fifty pounds, smooth, bald-headed glob-ular, baby-looking kind of guy. A giant baby. If you put him in a diaper, he would look perfectly at home.

He came up to a bunch of folks who were waiting in a chow line waiting to be fed. They were all *high* on the magic of that they're here at the collective, and they're going to get to eat. He came up and said,

"Oh, are you going in to eat? Oh, I *do* hope there's enough."

We had folks who actually put folks on about psychedelic things. I got put on by people a fair number of times, because I was so gullible and such a sucker to learn something. We wanted to learn something so bad. I remember distinct put-ons.

One of them I didn't really understand how much I had been put on until I saw the same person do it again to someone else.

This girl told me she could see my aura. I said, "Yeah? What's it like?"

She told me kind of a color range, and as she did, I thought, Well, if I'm aware of feeding back, maybe I can do a little better. So I tried to like clean house inside, straighten up a little, see if I could make it look better, and she said, "Oh. It brightened up when you did that," and told me that the colors had come up a little bit.

I went through that change with her a few times, and it was like trying to tune myself according to some feedback. Later on, I saw her doing it to a guy up at Harbinger, and I realized that she was putting him on. I realized that she had been putting *me* on, that she hadn't been able to see anything at all. She'd had me there posing for her, and straightening up and all that, and she couldn't see anything at all, except whatever I was revealing of my subconscious by whatever I did when she told me she could see my aura. Got put on pretty heavily by a seventeen-year-old-girl at that point.

Acid is very democratic that way. Non-ageist. Non-sexist. Et cetera. Who's tough is who's tough, and never mind.

I saw another example of that kind of put-on thing up at Harbinger. People always used to talk about what they could *see*. I'd sit around and I'd think,

Man, are these folks nuts, or what do they see? I don't even feel stoned. I'm bored and wish I was somewhere else, and these folks say they are having visions. I wonder where this is at.

There were these two guys who especially did a lot of that. They would say that they could see angels. And they would verify each other. One would say,

"Look how he's like this. And his thing's this way and he turns like this, and his color's that," and all that, and the other guy would agree. And everybody would say,

"Wow! Far out!"

I got a letter in the mail from that guy, some eight or nine years down the line from those events. He said,

"I saw you up at Harbinger. I was the guy, you might remember, who always used to talk about the angels and stuff. You know, I never really saw any of that stuff. Other people used to say they could see things, and I wondered. I thought, well, I should see things if they could see things. I couldn't see the things they saw, I figured they couldn't see mine either. I could say whatever I wanted, and then this other guy started backing me up. We became friends to back each other up, and neither one of us really ever saw anything."

I feel sorry for all those folks who used to sit around and believe those guys were having visions and seeing things when they weren't even having hallucinations. It's not a question of whether their hallucinations were true. They weren't even.

All the hotshots came up there to try to take over the place, because it was obvious that H. was not running it. He wasn't smart enough to be running it, and that made all the hotshots on Haight Street all think they could go out, and have it.

But it was still fun to go up and see the magicians, and watch them work out. They would come in, armed to the teeth with astral ammunition. Curly Jim came in armed with a heavy weight bass guitar, amplifier, and a mess of STP. He was rolling joints for people, with STP sprinkled in joints. Someone who got a hit on one of them described it as like being fired out of a cannon with a Byzantine barrel. But it left a lot of karma around. And eventually, Curly Jim moved up into one of the empty rooms in that old hundred room hotel, where they had walls knocked out of rooms and rooms in a row, and set up his amp and began to lay down loud, hard and heavy electronic, weird rock and roll, which boomed through the entire place. One thing while Curly Jim was there, you didn't forget he was there.

And at the same time, I have seen some weird stuff. But up there a lot of the stuff I saw was a little dark-arts flavored.

I saw H. lecture up there one time. The place sprouted out with pictures of him three feet high, full face pictures of great bald-headed baby face, looked like a nude or something. And then the next time, the place sprung out in big signs with big pink hearts on them saying stuff like *We love our Director!*

And the next visit, you come up to the place and you find all those signs smashed to flinders up against a concrete wall somewhere.

When H. lectured, Martha cried so bad that we had to carry her a mile and a half down the road, out of range of the p.a. enough before she would quit screaming. She hated to hear him talk on the p.a. It made her kick and scream and cry and raise hell. She just *hated* it.

H. was talking in a doorway, and the microphone was suspended above him in such a way that, with its great big old rubber windsock on it blocking out the light, his face was completely in the dark. Hanging over the top of the doorway behind him, as the altar cloth for that meeting, was a cow's hide, black and white spots, irregular.

No symmetry.

It was not a good meeting.

It's funny how the symbols around an event will reflect the event. But it's not funny at all, because the event is the symbols around it, too. That's what makes the event be the event. This is merely describing some of the event. It's not saying *This is not real*, or *This is supernatural*, but it's talking about something real. It's saying, Here. This is an event. And these are the factors that come out at you; and the flavor of the event is what causes these to be the factors that come out at you—they are the event.

It was tremendously valuable to watch Harbinger. The project could have succeeded. Harbinger could have been twelve, fifteen years old by now, in California. 1600 acres. But it ain't.

H. said stuff that sounded so weird, totalitarian and strange, that I wondered,

What are all these people doing up here?

This was one place where I learned what kind of stuff people can do with one another. After he got done talking, the people broke up in little groups, and stood in little groups with their arms around each other, and started om-ing together and talking together in little groups with their arms around one another, as hippies like to do—stand in circles like that and talk—and as they did that, he wanted to make it look like they were still doing what he said. There's a certain kind of magician who does that: tells you to do what you're already doing, so it looks like they're telling you what to do. He said,

"That's right. Stand there in your security groups."

Security groups.

Oh, you college psychologist, you! Oh, you bad college head-copper! Oh, you institutional schizophrenic mind-grabber, you!

A great experiment went down the tubes on weirdity there.

Their trip was that trip that a lot of people ask and want to know about. The only income they had was the new people throwing in their stuff. That's how that kind of collectivity got a bad reputation. They had to be continually fleecing and bilking a succession of new folks out of their bread to be able to keep their budget going.

I hung out there a little bit and looked at it. I thought

maybe I should try to straighten it. And I did try to straighten it some, but...

It was as if there was a larceny fad. There was so many head-coppers up there. I went up to play the action. It was like Las Vegas for telepaths. That's what we all went up there for, was to play the action.

There was one little building one time, that had some kind of machine in it that H. had made. It had a bar of non-conducting material about three-quarters of an inch around, and about six feet long, with copper coil wrapped around it, and you were supposed to come and aim this thing at you somewhere, and plug it in, and throw the switch. It was called the Zendyne Zapper. Folks said you could really get a high off the Zendyne Zapper. And the vibes around it were very paranoid and Frankensteiny.

I went up there several times. I had one trip in the hot baths, where a San Francisco dealer gave me a lump of peyote tar. I ate it, and went up into the hot bath. The hot bath was *hot*. I don't know what the temperature was, but it was *hot*. It took all of your concentration to just inch into it, inch by inch. And once you were into it, you had to stand perfectly still, because if you moved, you dissipated your little sheath of cool around you, and let it touch you again. It was *hot*.

I came out of that still coming on to this lump of peyote tar the size of the end of my thumb. I went out into the next room, where they had a big body-temperature pool. I climbed into that pool, and there was a lady there who I'll always remember, a beautiful, strong-looking lady. She picked me up by the head, and let me know that she wouldn't let me drown, and told me to just go on ahead and just let it hang out.

The windows were painted over in the room where the pool was, so it was pretty dark grey in the room. The water in the pool was body-temperature, and this lady was holding my head up so I wouldn't sink, and I was doing full-lung, full-body *om's*. As full as I could pull in, then out all the way, as hard as I could go. I don't know how long I did that, but at some point I sort of *beached* up on the edge of the pool. I crawled out and sat down on a curb.

I was sitting there with my elbows on my knees on a low curb, with no clothes on, looking at my crotch and my feet. And after a long time, I realized that what I was looking at was my crotch and my feet. It was me; those were my feet; that was my crotch. There I was, and that was what I had been looking at. But I had looked long minutes of unrecognition at these simple objects.

I must have been pretty spaced at that point. Then a guy came along and laid a nice one on me. He was an organic gardener, and he said,

"I know what you're trying to do, and want you to always know I'm a friend of yours, and want to help you out."

I was there one night when I don't know how many cops came. There was an amazing number of cops. There was a big jam going on, with hundreds of hippies from the Bay Area boogieing and partying and doing their thing, and suddenly there was heat all *over* the place.

Gavin Arthur, the grandson of President Chester A. Arthur, was there, an astrologer who spent some time at Harbinger. I watched him go through an ego death on acid, dosed and thinking that he was really dying, and telling all his students what to do with his possessions, and how to run the *ashram* after he was gone. I told him that I'd taken a lot of acid, and that he was just having an ego death, and it was cool and all that stuff, but he didn't want to hear it. He was having a good trip and didn't want to change it.

I talked to Tarthang Tulku for a short time. I soon discovered that all he was really interested in was finding somebody who would front him to print his old Tibetan texts. He was absolutely single-minded about that, and did not give a hoot for anything else that was going on. When

240

he determined that I wasn't going to do that, he was done with me, and he dismissed me.

But I wasn't done with *him* yet. I wanted to know some more about tulkus. So I hollered at him and made him turn back to me, and ran him through a few more questions before I let him go.

That was at the Great Harbinger Bust, where the giant hippie commune, hundreds of people, got raided. There were cops from all over the place. Ron T. was drunk. He came up the steps slurring,

"Gonna kill a pig!"

And he ran right smack into a great big one, one about foot and a half taller than him; and while he was kind of woozily looking at that, trying to figure out what to do, the cop who had overheard him looked down at him and said, kind of compassionately,

"Not very smart, are you?"

They locked us in an upstairs room, and locked some of us in a downstairs room, and I started raising hell about having my kid with me. So I just did that until I got Dana brought up.

One of the old *espontaneos* from Marin County was there—all that money until his family took it away from him with a conservatorship, used to run *big* acid parties in Marin County, PCP, THC, another one who claimed to be the Emperor on the Tarot Deck. Anyway, he started taking off all his clothes, and throwing this weird scene on the people there, took off all his clothes, which was making the cops look at us like we were a bunch of ding-a-lings. He was deeply into the juice. There were fifty or a hundred people in the room, whose character he was wrecking by the second as he went.

He was throwing his bod around. He was about six-foot-six, and some folks didn't want to look, and some folks were fascinated. He was scaring people with some kind of body vibe trip. I saw what he was doing, and I thought that if he could throw his bod around, I could throw mine around. So I ran over to him, threw my arms around his neck, and just threw a melt on him.

"Yechhhh!!"

He recoiled.

I just hung on him in a complete melt.

Then I turned around to the other people in the room. I said,

"Lookie here, this looks like hell, the way this has been going down. Why don't we just sit down, straighten up, smart up, get thinking quietly, meditate here a little about what's happening to us."

Everybody bought that, and changed our thing.

I really *wanted* to change the thing around and make it so there was better vibes than them searching us all in the room—because I had been holding, and half my party was holding.

They were collective about some stuff, but they weren't at all collective about some other stuff. They weren't collective about troubles. You could go there and throw everything you had in the pot, but if you got in trouble, there wasn't anybody there who was going to take care of you, because they weren't collective about their troubles, that was different. They were collective with their new folks' new stuff. Hard way to survive.

The king and the queen knew they weren't any king and queen. They were some nice, ordinary folks who got stuck with those chairs. And they weren't talking for the kings and queens, anyway. What they meant was that the heavy ego people and the high-profile, big noise folks had taken over the place so bad that the majority of folks who wanted to come here and be collective couldn't do it, because there was too heavy a scene going down. We saw that a scene like that, if it was going to succeed, had to in some way be protective of the people who didn't want to be high-profile and big noise. It had to be so that the biggest mouth couldn't just walk in and walk away with all the energy all the time, or it wouldn't be fair. It wasn't fair at Harbinger, and the place—although they had lots of money, and nice land and a hundred-room hotel, and hot springs and swimming pool and all that—deteriorated to where the people didn't get any protection, so they went away. And when they went away, it fell apart real fast. They had all mouths to feed and no hands to work, and had become a hummingator commune— the mouth of an alligator and the body of a hummingbird.

The Commons Meetings

There was a series of meetings that took place when the light show guys went on strike. They were striking against Chester and Graham, mainly. The guy from the light shows was saying that light shows were as heavy as bands, and should get equal billing and equal money, and was pushing for that kind of thing. And nobody really thought that was true, but he got a lot of light show guys believing that, or hopped up on that enough that they went out in front of the Family

Dog on the Great Highway with all their light show projectors, and they were throwing their light shows on the front of it, like *projecting their images against it.* Heavy magic.

The light show guy was just as hot as Fidel Castro, stirring up revolution. Chester dug it as an energy flux, and was going to see what he could do with it. Graham was insulted, and was going to put the revolution down immediately.

There followed some meetings out of this that became known as the Commons. The Commons were kind of funny meetings, because all the guys who were the heavyweights in the community, the bands and like that, would all sit around and figure out what they were going to do, trying to figure out a way to make it, so everybody could have a share of it, and like that. So Chester thought he had really done what he had to do, taking that strike and turning that energy around into productive meetings.

We were at one of those meetings, and Leary came in all about he was going to run for governor; and he was going to do a big pitch about that. That was the reason we'd taken him home to my house one time—to try to talk him out of running for governor. We saw that we were going to be back-to-back. We had a class party scheduled for Wednesday night at the Family Dog, and Leary had gotten the Dog for Thursday night, to throw his On-for-Governor trip in.

I thought about that, and I didn't like it. I tried to figure out what to do about it, and I realized that what to do was to make a three day jam. Add another day, Friday, to the trip, and throw a three-day scene—I would do some of it, and Leary would do some of it; we'd invite all the teachers we could think of, and we'd throw a big scene there—which I was throwing to surround this Leary-for-Governor scene, because it was such a dumb idea and it was messing with the energy. It was really an elitist kind of a trip, coming down the pyramid, and I was being revolutionary about that.

I went to Chester and I said,

"Chester, How about this?" Chester dug it, and immediately went and told the Commons. They bought it, and we threw the Holy Man Jam.

After it was over, they were all blown. Chester came and said,

"Holy Man Jam. Good business!"

And they tried to throw a series of them. Other people tried to throw them after that. Several more went off around the Holy Man Jam, because it had gotten off so good.

Another time, at one of those meetings, somebody came in with a lid of super dope, and Garcia and his friends were over there, and the back end of the Dog turned into a giant marble Roman or Greek meeting forum type thing, and we were all in Togas, and we just had to sort it out for a while. It got outrageous, as we smoked that lid of super dope in about fifteen minutes among the people who were there.

This series of meetings was going on, and the real bad blood was between the light show guy and Bill Graham. That was where the fight had started. So even though the meetings were going to happen and all that was going on, that hassle still kept going on, and didn't get settled. Graham stepped out in the middle of a circle, maybe fifty people in a circle, maybe thirty or forty feet across, some standing, some sitting, some squatting around, pieces of stage scattered here and there, people piled up on that,...and Graham steps into the middle of the circle, and the agreement is that everybody's going to get to say their thing.

So Graham starts talking, and he's just putting it severely on the light show guy, who's a very proud, paranoid, uptight, and incredibly angry dude at this point. And Graham is just putting it on him laying it on him, making him out an ass, taunting and jeering at him, knowing exactly where he's at—Graham, an intelligent and proud and strong man of full growth, doing this to this dude.

I saw that, and I thought it was weird and perverse for

Graham to be pushing that cat that way in that situation. I knew that light show guy and I knew he was capable of almost anything, if he was angry enough. He did that to the light show guy for minutes, and it wound the whole meeting up like a coiled spring with incredible tension in it, with that cat sitting there, and some people, me mostly, knowing where he was at about anger.

Graham got done chewing, and the light show guy was going to be the next to speak. And before he spoke, I jumped up and said,

"I want to say something here. May I have permission to say something at this point? There is something that needs to be said at this point."

That started a dogfight, in that tension, for me to do that. The fight went on, and just raged for about fifteen or twenty minutes. There were guys in the back who were for me, yelling out,

"Let the cat in the purple pants talk, man."

And other people saying,

"Ah, shaddup, Stephen. Siddown!" And stuff like that.

I hung on and argued it out until the meeting settled to a place where they said,

"All right. What do you want to say?"

And I said,

"Actually, I don't have anything to say. But I didn't like what Graham was doing to him, and I didn't like the amount of tension that had been stored up on the light show guy before he was going to answer, and I thought it was going to make for some real bad vibes, so I just took this excuse to defuse it,..."

Some people started laughing and clapping their hands. Others started booing, saying,

"Aw, shit!"

About half and half. Half of them thought it was really funny, and half of them were just really mad, that I should do such a thing.

Later on in the same meeting, things had passed a bit, and Graham came out and was going to run another shot. He stepped out in the middle and said,

"You know, I used to go to acting school, man, I was going to be an actor, man, I was going to be the next Eli Wallach." And he marked out a little stage on the floor, suggesting the dimensions of a stage he might be standing on with a couple of waves of his hand.

"And I might do a thing like this,..." and he started doing it. And I saw him rev. He just revved, and got going. He talked about how he'd been *messed* with, and how much *trouble* he'd had, and how hard it was for him to manifest, and what fools a bunch of folks were, and he cried and he raged and he roared, and just really threw an acting-school fit, right there on the stage. And I *knew* it was an acting school fit, and he was putting all these people through these changes. When he slowed for a breath, a pretty gentle hippy who used to babysit for Janis Joplin said that whatever Graham was doing, it was for the money, anyhow.

Graham just blew. Brrrrmmmmmmcccchhhhhhh!

He completely flew off the handle, angry, mad, at being messed with a second time in one day. He started walking out. The gentle hippy walked up to Graham as he was going out the door, and cuddled up next to him, put his hand on his shoulder and tried to calm him, and said,

"*Bill...*"

And Bill spun around, and said,

"DON'T ... TOUCH ... ME!!!"

And froze him in that shape, and walked out the door, leaving him standing there curved around an empty silhouette of Bill Graham.

By that time, the room was so electric that three ten-year old black kids walking down the street in front of the Family Dog, threw four feet of lead pipe in through the glass of the front window.

San Francisco Holy Man Jam

 n one of the nights at the Holy Man Jam, it was Alan Watts' night to gig. We were up in the Performers' Room, and it was Malachi and his guys, three of them who wore Tibetan robes. One of them wore white brocade and looked like a baby. We always joked that Malachi was keeping the Dalai Lama on the side there. They wore all Tibetan stuff and did Tibetan prayer wheels that required you to concentrate on the thing. Little balance things...

249

Also the Phoenix was there, banged on a lot of acid. Alan walked in and looked around the room at all the people and said,

"Look at these people. Look what this room is full of. These are *monks*. Why, these are monks." And came on like that.

And Malachi looked up and said,

"Hey, Alan! You want a *radong?*"

A *radong* is a seven-foot long Tibetan horn that makes the kind of intestinal squeaks and thonks of Tibetan music.

Alan says,

"I can't play a *radong!*"

"I got a *radong-ist*," says Malachi, who was from Texas.

Alan said it might be all right to have a little *radong*.

I said,

"Hey, if you're gonna blow horn, how about I blow this horn, too?"

He said, "Sure. Let's blow that one, too."

So we went on stage, everybody who had a horn. Alan sat up to do his gig, and the rest of us just thought we'd give him a little boost, and help his gig go over good. It was like blowing rhythm, or side man or something for him. We got on the back, and Malachi's *radong*-ist, and me and my cow horn and some other horns, and we just blew great long billowing bursts into all these folks. Then Alan started talking, and it was the best I ever saw him.

He started telling them, and he was telling them where it was at. It was clear and it was clean. Somebody started talking in the back of the room, and he said,

"Stop that talking in the back of the room. This is no time for that. We're here for something." He straightened him up, man. I never ever saw him do that, before or again. He looked so good, and it felt so good, that it made the hall just relax—*whew! Somebody's in charge. Somebody's going to help out.* He was good. He did his lick. I was never sorry that I went onstage with him, me and Malachi's *radong*-ist.

There was this guy who was a certified bad-ass in San Francisco, Panda Bear. He hung out with the Hell's Angels. Panda Bear once put a kilo price on somebody's head, to get them beat up. Chester and I were the only two who stepped out into the circle and spoke out against that.

We were in the Performers' Room of the Theater during the Holy Man Jam. I think I was on acid; Leary was there, and he was on acid; Rolling Thunder was there, and he was eating peyote; Chester was there, probably on acid; and Panda Bear was there, on a lot of stuff, some of which was coke, and I don't know what else. And he had the leaps—the coke leaps—real heavy rushes. There were drummers who were famous for their coke rushes: br-r-r-r-r-r-m-m-m-m-t-t-t-t-t!!!

Panda Bear was ripping everybody off pretty hard. Panda Bear was not his real name. His real name was *Ursulus horribilis*. He was a grizzly bear. He was not a Panda Bear. And he was roaring with his coke rushes. He would roar so loud, and so psychedelically loud, that he would just blanket everybody with just **roarrr!**

Rolling Thunder was trying to do magic at him to make him cool it. Rolling Thunder would spit in his hand and hit it with his fist, looking over at Panda—to short circuit these coke rushes he was having.

What I was doing was, I thought,

"I am not going to fight these coke rushes." But when Panda Bear would rush and when he would go on his roar, I'd put my arm around his shoulders and just *hang* there, and melt on him and be real soft, and just ride on the roar, as soft and as yin as I could be, while he would roar. And as soon as he would get done roaring, I would brace back up into myself, and be strong, and do something salty with him. Everybody else would be shattered by his roar, trying to find out where in the world they were, because it was so psychically devastating; but I would be riding with him on his roar, and I would jump off just before he took a breath;

and I would be the only one who was in good shape while he was catching a breath. Then I would do something sarcastic and magical to try to diminish the effect of his magic by doing something like offering him a joint and saying,

"Would you like a hit?" while he's trying to catch his breath in between roars.

We went through some changes in that room. Chester lay down in the middle of the circle because he needed to lay down a little bit, and someone started leching on Chester's bod, and threw that vibe into the meeting so hard and into everybody's head, until Chester said,

"Well, I've just got to get up and remove the temptation," and he got up and got out of the circle and went back over to the side again.

I left, and to go out of there you went through a great, big, dark, empty room, with a staircase that went downstairs. It had a couple of windows in the front of it, out over the dance floor.

When I got out into that room, Panda Bear came for me. He was roaring, and coming on heavy to me, by myself out in this dark room.

He came up next to me, and reached for a roar. As he reached for it, I did something completely out of character for me—I just slapped my hand sort of gently on his stomach—he had his shirt off, and he was very hairy. I wound my fingers up in his stomach hair, and *jerked*.

It brought him up short, cut him off in mid roar, essentially took his energy-chi and disoriented him. I left him upstairs and went downstairs. The Ashoke Fakir was on stage.

When the Ashoke Fakir introduced his family to the crowd at the Holy Man Jam at the Family Dog, they exuded a kind of unctuous embarrassment as they came onstage to be introduced, because his anxiousness to introduce his family to that crowd brought the secret too close to the surface: that although he was the Indian Holy Man, it was the crowd who had the juice. And although he was the Indian Holy Man and was demonstrating energy, he brought his family before the crowd for *their* blessing. And the two levels of secret almost broke free at that point, and it embarrassed everybody just a little bit. There were fifteen hundred, two thousand people there. Probably seven hundred of them were on acid.

A guy named Jerry Jarvis from Transcendental Meditation got up and put down acid, and they were all polite, and didn't boo him or hiss him or anything, just sat there and let him have his say while he mouthed off this amazing jive about acid. People would just look at each other and smile, while he talked all this nonsense. And we all thought, and it was perfectly telepathic through the hall, *Look at that dude, in his suit, sitting there, surfing on seven hundred people's vibes who are high on acid, and putting acid down while he is riding on acid power while he talks.*

Antonio's Tai Chi teacher, a mean Chinese cat, tall and austere, dressed in black, had a small wife in a permanent cringe who walked several feet behind him. He taught Tai Chi and General Arrogance. For part of his thing at the Holy Man Jam, he did a demonstration of Tai Chi swordfighting with a great, long, double-edged sword, three feet long, an inch and a half wide, shiny silver. He did that kind of Tai-Chi sword play with it on the stage; and there were people sitting around at the edge of the stage on the amplifiers, at the foot and the back of the stage, and they were within feet, sometimes inches, of the sword as he whirled it around. It scared those people so hard that everybody froze for yards and yards away from the stage, afraid to make a move in case he should make a mistake with his blade. Scared those people up their tree with his old Tai Chi.

He was standing on the stage in a white silk flowing shirt and this big sword, sort of strutting and preening. When I saw what he had done, and how badly he had scared the audience, and how much energy he had gotten from it I said, loud and authoritatively,

"*And at the other end of the room, we are going to set up for the next show.*" And everybody in the room turned around and faced the back of the room, and left him standing there on the stage looking at a lot of people's backs. And there wasn't in fact anything going on at the back of the room. I had thought there was going to be, but there wasn't.

Some people thought I was just an ass for misdirecting the crowd that way. But in my universe, it looked to me like he had scared a bunch of people who were pretty stoned, pretty badly with that blade. And I just moved that juice off of him and back to the people.

Some people were good there, too.

In a way, of all the people who came to the Holy Man Jam in San Francisco, Satchidananda did what was advertised on the poster more than anyone else. It turned into the eliminations, which was not what was advertised on the poster. But Satchidananda came in, and he gave a religious experience, which was advertised on the poster.

Satchidanada showed some of his chanting expertise at that time. He chanted the *Om shantih, om shantih.* He chanted it so sweet, and held them for so long that they just turned into pure tones in the room, and the whole room would just freeze. And he'd let it go into complete silence. Then, at the first sign of a sound, of a rustle in the auditorium, before that sound could generate loud enough to affect anyone's mind, he would come off the line, and outdraw that noise, and go into the next movement of his chant.

A lot of folks didn't even know. But some folks saw what he was doing, and just thought he was *very cool.* He'd hit that *om shantih* and rev it up again sweet and nice, the way a really sweet chanter can, and do it again. So he really gave a religious experience at the San Francisco Holy Man Jam. Most of the folks there were fairly severely into the juice, I think.

Nitrous With Chester

hester had a friend with a Cadillac who would occasionally pretend to be a chaffeur when Chester wanted to do a deal. They were off on a scam together, and I went along for the ride.

We went over to Chester's rich friend's house who's going to come up with some money to help open the Family Dog. As we came in I noticed there was a funny collection of people in the house. Some young, some old, black and white, mixed group. And there was this one guy who was apparently very rich. He was treated with a certain deference, almost like fear. And I also noticed that above the fireplace nailed to the wall was an actual two-horned devil mask as the central object of the room. I wondered what kind of a place it might be.

While Chester was negotiating, someone whirled into the house with a five-foot tall green tank of nitrous oxide. The millionaire began saying,

"Ah hah, we gonna have nitrous tonite, ah hah."

He began preparing the tank to hit on. As the tank was there people were warned to be careful and don't take it too quick off the tube, don't freeze their lungs. Everybody hit up on it and we began to go into a weird strange nitrous level where reality and the sound moved in great *Wowwww, Wowwwww*, waves like strange synthesizer noises. The entire consciousness was being wowwwwed back and forth.

I saw that the millionaire was an old time nitrous tripper because he would speak sentences dropping one word and then a big *wowwwww* of the entire consciousness and then he would say the next word of the sentence and drop one word in each *wowwww*.

The black lady looked a little concerned and said,

"Oh do promise us you will be good to us tonite, please."

The millionaire said,

"Hee, hee, hee. I'm a son-of-a-bitch on nitrous. Hah, hah, hah."

Chester and I and the millionaire were passing the hose off the nitrous tank. It looked to me as if the millionaire was doing something to Chester's mind out in the nitrous astral. It didn't look good to me. It looked like Chester was so banged he was a little undefended, and this guy was not being good to him.

I grabbed Chester by the arm and we walked out of the house down the sidewalk, got in the back of the Cadillac. I told the driver to go on. We were half a block down the street before Chester came off of the nitrous enough to ask,

"What are we doing in the car? Where are we going?"

I told him what had happened and he was somewhat angered with me, and he didn't think he needed the protection. But, from where I was looking, into the sight of both their minds, it didn't look like a good thing was happening.

You always had to be careful how you took care of your mind.

Nitrous had a strange reputation as being a drug that caused a certain amount of competition. When you hit on nitrous it lifts you a little ways and then you drop pretty quick, then it lifts you a little ways and then you drop pretty quick. Then you come to a place as Psychedelic Bob said, the Gateless Gate, and you want to maintain that, so you have to hit again. And people sometimes get competitive then, over who's going to hit. Feelings get a little rough over who's going to maintain the highest consciousness.

The feeling in the body was an excruciating tickle that felt funny and good to the tips of my toes, and the ends of my fingernails, and the ends of my hair.

Boulder Holy Man Jam

he way it really worked was, I heard that Swami Satchidananda was staying in this house, and I was going to try to have this meeting with him. When I got there, Yogi B. was parked in front of the house in his Jag. I just went on into the house, and Satchidananda was waking up and coming out of a back room.

He came out and called me a good shepherd. He put his arms around me and hugged me and called me his son, and

258

looked at me and be'd completely androgynous, and told me I was beautiful and that he loved me.

Suddenly, the door *slammed* back open, and Yogi Bhajan came *striding* in the door, which banged the wall from the force of his slamming it open—because he knew I was in there with Satchidananda, and he didn't dig it. He came blasting into the room and he says,

"And the movie rights, Swami. What are we going to do about the movie rights?"

And Satchidananda gets himself together very quick as if caught smooching with the maid, and suddenly snaps away from me, and doesn't allow himself to be seen in the loving position he'd been in with me when Yogi B. walked into the room. It was across caste lines, and he couldn't be seen doing it.

Yogi Bhajan says,

"What have you been doing?"

And Satchidananda said,

"I was in the other room, in an *unconscious* state. Ho-ho-ho. Sure is hot, isn't it?"

And Yogi Bhajan said,

"Haven't you taught them how to fan a *guru* yet?"

Then we sat, the three of us in the room, in a triangle, knee-to-knee, all of us in the Lotus position, and all of our knees touching, the three of us. I realized that we *were* an energy center that was holding one of the bearing points of the juice. And I thought,

It is some kind of an honor to be included in this trinity as part of this bearing point and hold this juice; but the next time I'm in one of these things, the other two parts are going to be on my team, too.

It was very stoned for a bit, and it was very quiet. We talked a little, and they asked me if I wasn't going to come over and tell folks to get off psychedelics.

I told them that I didn't think I could and that I still found value in it.

We didn't come to any agreements about it.

I was a hangup to them, because I had a lot of juice, and was psychedelic-powered. The only trouble with psychedelic power was that it was running *wild,* and it didn't belong to nobody's Establishment. It was running *wild.*

They couldn't hack that. They had thousands of years invested. That was why Satchidananda could open himself up to me when we were alone—because I was stoned, and young and clean—but when Yogi B. came in, he had to snap back to what the Establishment might think about it.

He got his swami papers from the swami school. There's probably a head swami around.

After we came out of the house, Yogi B. had gotten back in his Jag, and I walked over to him and he tried to hypnotize me. He had a handful of turquoise rings on, and he started waving his hands in these hypnotic passes in front of my face, and coming on to me very head-on, forceful, frontwards, a lot of domination, a lot of will at me. And I didn't cop to it, but I was somewhat offended that someone should attempt to get my gourd by actual frontal assault.

There's a real good value in going back up into your monk's cell, and getting your act together, and getting seriously into yourself and spending maybe years if you have to, to do it. But there are also international, inter-plane pirates and sorcerers out on the world, doing stuff. I'm talking about magic I have seen go down at other times, but these are the times of Jim Jones and the Ayatollah—who are really only explainable with some kind of magic.

A lot of the guys in this book are my real teachers. They are who taught me my stuff. When somebody says, "Who's your teacher," some people think it means, "Do you wear Ford on your baseball hat, or do you wear General Motors on your baseball hat?" But it means who really taught you your stuff. And these guys are my real teachers. In a way, this is all obeisance to the gurus.

The kind of thing you learned from people like Patrick M. was how to keep your attention one-pointed and focused, so you could continue to do something while circumstances would tend to dissolve your concentration and make you unable to finish your thought trains. The stuff I learned from Patrick, in good measure, helped when I was up at nine thousand feet at Brainerd Lake at the Boulder Holy Man Jam, and Yogi Bhajan was sitting on a bunch of rocks holding court.

When I arrived at the top of the hill, there were a few hippies taking off their clothes and jumping in the lake. And Yogi B. and his crew didn't approve of it. They were so strong psychically that their disapproval of it manifested in that all the boobs looked draggy and saggy and unpretty, and all the peckers looked veiny and warty and weird looking, and it all looked like not-very-pretty pornography, instead of just the ordinary bodies of some ordinary people who were jumping in a lake.

I could see that manifestation, and I knew it wasn't cool.

One of the people who was there was Michel, a French magician from commune *La Hermaphrodite* in Southern France, in his long cape and cloak and black eyepatch. There was another dude who was a tall, heavy-duty, well set-up cat, wearing Levi shorts and hiking boots and nothing else, who spoke your subconscious in iambic pentameter, and declaimed like a Shakespearean actor, in a very stentorian style, a lot of what was in your head. He was telepathic, and the state he put himself in was like an automatic poetry state, and he would just babble; and he would babble whoever's head he was nearest to. What happened to a lot of people was, as soon as they heard it they became fascinated by it and zeroed in on it, and gave him the keys to the safe. And he would proceed to pick the lock and suck up all their juice while he had them.

As I came up the hill, I was greeted by Michel, who was screaming,

"Get off of this hill! This is *my* hill! You have no right to come up here. It is my hill; you have no reason to be up here. *Get off of this hill!"*

At the same time, I cross paths with the Shakespearean declaimer, and I think,

Well, I can't hassle with Michel like this while I'm all this stoned—I was eating some peyote.

So I stepped over in between them, and I threw my attention into the Shakespearean declaimer. He began to turn up loud and confident and real noisy, and took over until hardly anyone could talk over him, because he had such a good strong set of lungs and mouth, and I was just there socking it to him and giving him everything I had to talk. And he out-talked Michel, who was talking other bad talk I didn't want to listen to.

The whole scene continued to compound on and weird out because it was not very well taken care of. I went over to the rocks where the Yogi Bhajan entourage was sitting, and Michel was over there, deep into the juice. One of Yogi B.'s ladies was there in white dress and white turban. At one point, Michel reached out and slapped her alongside the chops.

One of Yogi B.'s young lieutenants immediately stepped forth and took him in a fast judo throw and took him down on his back and had him down on the ground, *instantly.*

Michel melted, and at a weird instant, telepathic, transfixed moment, everybody stood around in a circle and looked down at this guy holding Michel down, and Michel vibed, very strong, very clearly. It was as if it was said:

Please don't pick up my eye patch!

I started hollering at the cat to let him up, he wasn't going to hit anybody else, he was already defused, he was off his trip, he had been scared. The cat told me to shut up, and I hollered back at him. He stood up and told me,

"I don't know what *you* were when *you* were in the service, but *I* was an officer!"

I went back over to the edge to wait. Somebody gave me some peyote. I stood in the middle of a big crowd of people, and I started taking bites off of peyote buttons, and it began to rain, and we began to get stoned, and know that we were hippies together, and that it was cool, it was all right. We stood in a circle and ate big fat juicy green buttons, and it rained on us and we looked up in the sky and cried and the tears mixed with the rain that ran down us all, and we were all really blessed and cool and nice on the hilltop.

Upon walking back down the mountain, I was followed by Michel, back into my case again, on one end, and Yogi B. on the other, whom I ran into and gave a few smartass parting remarks—just to be ritually disrespectful—and went on down to the bottom of the hill, and split the Boulder jam.

Michel was another one of those guys who was a scary magician to some folks; but if you really understood where he was at, he was another one of those hyper-shellshocked pacifists.

Guys would come back from trips so humble that they weren't sure if the amount of oxygen they were breathing was cool, in the larger scheme of things. What *were* they worth, if anything?

Thank God I'm a hippy.

It saved me.

That's not a fanciful word.

Saved.

As in prevented-from-being-a-total-waste.

Saved.

Kept from being lost and useless.

Kent State, Dosed:

got to a place where I liked where I was at pretty well. It was a real shaky time out in the world. What was going on all around was real shaky. I felt like I would rather just be solid through this next period of time, than trip. I had built one that I believed in pretty good, and I quit taking acid. I let folks know.

I also quit grass for several months: everything, including grass, for several months one time. And then I started smoking grass again.

The day the students got shot at Kent State was Monday. There was an old acid dealer who knew that it had been nine months since I had taken any acid. He wasn't particularly thinking that this was the night that the students got shot at Kent State or anything, he was on his own trip. He said he wanted to see if I was still honest. So he had his little girl go up and give me some candy. And it had four or five hundred mikes of good acid on it. As I ate it, the little girl let me know. She said,

"Ooops, psychedelic!"

I ate it up. I had taken a big bite off it, and had a little piece of it left, which I popped into my mouth. Might as well get the rest of it. Once you're over the edge, at that point, you might as well have a good load.

I sat down and started doing class, talking and rapping. It came to the break, and I didn't really *know* I was dosed. It had just been a joke in a way. But when we came back from the break and we om-ed, I found myself floating loose. I opened my eyes and I was about six feet from the ceiling. I had astral projected clear out of my body, and was up on the top of this seventy-foot ceiling in this auditorium.

Then *Poof!* I was sucked back into my body instantly, as soon as I saw where I was. I thought, *I...am...stoned!...I... have...been...**dosed!***

In the second half, the militants made their move, and started coming on that there were all these thousands of people who came to talk to me, and listen, and that they ought to be into violent revolution. They said they were shooting us, and we had to consider violence at this point, because they were killing us. They had killed a bunch of us today at Kent State. At some point I said,

"I am so banged on acid that I don't really want to do this right now. Can I go?"

And the militants said,

"No. We aren't through talking about Kent State, and we

need to finish talking about that."

And we argued on for several more hours.

I was coming on very heavy to acid, and impassionedly arguing with these guys about this. At one point, I got almost scolding to some of the people there. It looked as though a lot of them were supporting that kind of violent attitude. I said·stuff like,

"I come in here and talk peace and love, and you guys say 'Yeah, yeah.' I come in here and I talk peace and love, and you guys say, 'Yeah, yeah.' I come in here and I talk peace and love, man, and..." And I was going to go off on "I talk peace and love and here you guys are coming on warlike." But instead of that, when I said it the third time, almost the entire room, it must have been ninety per cent, roared back at me,

"*Yeah! Yeah!*"

It was an incredible loud, strong consensus, and it took me off the hook. They cut me loose very free and very high.

It was that night, parked in our bus on the beach by Pacifica, where I went up a little farther in my mind and answered the old mail in my mailbox. I remembered an argument I had with a lady of my acquaintance named Renee. In the heat of the argument, I had said,

"There is something called the Void,...", and she had come back with,

"There is *nothing* called the Void."

I got stoned, and remembered her saying that to me, and saw how cleverly she had foxed me. Then I saw a couple more of those, like answering my mail since the last time I had been that stoned. They were places where people had come up and caught me on the rebound or on the blind side, and done a number on me, and they were just *fixed, right there*, at that level of consciousness, the next time I came back to that level to look at it, there it was. That was very funny, and it made me laugh. I knew I was had, but I also laughed.

I was sitting in the bus remembering that, very stoned. Ina May started crawling across the bed, and she suddenly became very ugly. I said,

"Stop that! What are you doing? Stop that!"

She stopped, and I started questioning her, what had she been *doing?* It looked so awful, terrible to look at.

"Actually," she said, "What happened was, I started to crawl across the bed to get something. I had a change of thought while I was moving, and I spaced out and forgot what I was going after. Then I thought, *I don't know what I'm going after.* And then I thought, *Well, I'll just keep crawling for a minute, and see if I remember.*"

She was crawling, going nowhere. She was expending energy to no purpose, and it was awful. It was bad to look at. It was unbeautiful. Truth is beauty and beauty is truth. Form and function, very psychic stuff.

For a while that evening I thought I could time-travel, by chanting *Echo echo echo echo echo echo,* as a mantra. As I speeded up and slowed down the speed of the mantra, I would slide up and down time lines, and drift in on people who were doing experiments to find out about telepathy. I would drop in on their experiments. Some folks had short brown beards and funny wireless looking trips, looked like 1890 mesmerists or something, European looking dudes. Other folks looked tribal. Whatnot. Visions in different places in time.

I felt a presentiment of anger from a friend, and knew that he was angry with me. It made me feel a cold, killer feeling in my body, as if I had my hand in a tray of ice cubes, and was sliding around in the tray of ice cubes, and some of them were sharp and were cutting me. I saw that friend the next day, standing on a clifftop. He had a pretty good size aura on—I guess partly because we'd been contacting seriously all night—but he also had a pretty good amount of juice. And his aura was torn as if the wind was blowing it. But the material wind doesn't move the psychic

267

plane. It was torn by some kind of psychic thing, and you could see that there was some kind of distress in his soul, from how his aura was peeled out into long tails and protuberances like comet tails, and tails of spiral nebulae and stuff, as energy shot off in different directions.

A friend of mine was in the hospital that day, and I had promised to go see him. He was a funny kind of dude. He was a very yang experience hound, a sensation hunter who liked a lot of everything, as much as he could get, and was always on the hustle to get a lot of that. The reason he was in the hospital was because of a series of karmic actions, which seemed correct, if not desirable. They produced the effect, very clearly. He had lifted a friend's motorcycle without permission. It wasn't like a theft, he was an old friend, who would just have said, why didn't you ask me or something like that. But he had lifted a friend's motorcycle to take a girl for a ride. In the course of taking her for a ride, he crossed paths at an intersection with a Cadillac from the Cadillac dealership, which was supposedly out on a demonstration ride, but which was actually being stolen, in the middle of a high speed chase across town. The Cadillac and the motorcycle intersected. The girl was not hurt, he got a broken leg and was banged up pretty good, but was all right. Nobody was hurt in the Cadillac, but the motorcycle and the Cadillac burst into flame and burned on the spot in the intersection, completely destroying both of them.

After all that, as I looked at him, the redness and juiciness of his mouth, and the rosiness of his cheeks made me know that on a deep, deep psychic level, he had dug it. He was still an experience hound, and he was not finished yet, and he would go out and look for some more when he got well from the last one, because he was that hard a sensation hunter. He didn't realize that the hunting he was doing for the sensations of sex and dope and booze and riding motorcycles and all that was the same desire that was calling up the wrecks and the fleeing robbers and the Cadillacs and the broken legs and flaming intersection and all that jive going down. He was manifesting up a sensational reality that he lived in.

I was still pretty stoned when I first walked into the hospital. One of the nurses looked at me as I came in the door and said,

"You can cheer up more than that." I was on a trip where I was going to not be on a trip in the hospital in order to not bug anybody. She took one look at me and said that. So I came back to normal, walked through and had fun looking at people in doors and watching their eyes and getting stoned with them, until I saw this dude. Then I had to think about that for a while.There he was, in traction, and not done yet. It made me understand that level of manifestation.

That was my last acid trip.

The End?

cid is like rock and roll, or making love. When you get out there into it, and you're really moving, you realize that it's been going on forever, and that you just check out of it temporarily. And when you come back to it, it's there, and it's been going on all the time while you were away from it. That's how acid is: when you come into it, it's been happening all the time. So there's no such thing as an old acid trip. Because acid trips don't have time anyway. They're just unsentimentally *now*.

When I began taking acid, it wasn't illegal to take acid. It was made illegal, somewhat because Tim Leary put on such a scary show to the California state legislature. I haven't taken acid for at least ten years, and I haven't done a serious tripping size amount of mushrooms or peyote in most of that time.

Everybody I knew who seriously tripped always felt that if you got your karma together, you wouldn't come down. And when you were coming down, sometimes you almost couldn't tell. It almost looked like you weren't coming down, if you didn't do any obvious bad-karma things, didn't get any of those sudden sinking sensations in the pit of your stomach that made you know you were losing a lot of altitude fast. If you didn't have anything like that happen, you might fool yourself along that you were still pretty stoned, although you might not be as stoned as you were.

But you only have to be moving a *little bit* to have steerageway. And steerageway is what you want. Without any motion, sometimes you lack direction. So you have a little bit of motion, just enough to give you steerageway in the medium.

In the material plane, as long as you have sufficient velocity, you have steerageway. But in the astral plane, velocity doesn't give it to you. The mind is capable of integrating anything, and it integrates a stable velocity; and if you are no longer accelerating in the psychic medium, you lose steerageway because of the mind's ability to integrate any stable medium, tone, feeling, sound or touch into nothing, like the feeling of your belt, or living by a waterfall, or the sixty-cycle hum, or being on ten cups of coffee.

Smoking grass gives you a little acceleration, and then you come down. At a relatively low level of karma, compared with what it takes to get accelerated with acid. Acid is like a heavy lift-off vehicle for lunar shots—but it's only a mile to town.

So you could run on grass, or no grass and good karma. Anything, just so as to keep moving a little bit. It wasn't that I had learned everything acid could teach me. But that particular set of contents in my head had been pretty scrambled and sorted and weighed and combed and computerized and run through and done over. If I was really ever going to have another significant benefit from a psychedelic as heavy as the ones that I had had, I would probably have to wait decades, and live a lot of lifetime, and make another whole store in there.

So, I'm laying up treasures where moth and rust do not corrupt, and just smoking enough grass now and then to get steerageway. And I may trip again some day.